The FOUR GOSPELS

The FOUR GOSPELS

Combined & Chronological

MARK P. KRIEGER

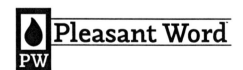

Pleasant Word (a division of WinePress Publishing, PO Box 428, Enumclaw, WA 98022) functions only as book publisher. As such, the ultimate design, content, editorial accuracy, and views expressed or implied in this work are those of the author.

Unless otherwise noted, all Scriptures are taken from the *Holy Bible, New International Version®, NIV®*. Copyright © 1973, 1978, 1984 by Biblica, Inc.™ Used by permission of Zondervan. All rights reserved worldwide. WWW. ZONDERVAN.COM

Scripture references marked KJV are taken from the *King James Version* of the Bible.

Scripture references marked NASB are taken from the *New American Standard Bible*, © 1960, 1963, 1968, 1971, 1972, 1973, 1975, 1977 by The Lockman Foundation. Used by permission.

ISBN 13: 978-1-4141-0908-4
ISBN 10: 1-4141-0908-3
Library of Congress Catalog Card Number: 2006910618

For God so loved the world that He gave His only
begotton Son ...

—John 3:16a

CONTENTS

Arrival of the Christ

PREFACE

Have you ever had the desire to read the four Gospels as one cohesive unit? I have—this writing is my attempt to combine Matthew, Mark, Luke, and John into one book in chronological order.

The text translation/paraphrase is the result of my extensive hermeneutic and exegetic study of the four Gospels. The chronology is based on the work found in *The Life and Times Historical Reference Bible* by Thomas Nelson, Inc., 1997. The "Introduction of the Four Gospels" was extracted from *The NIV Study Bible* by The Zondervan Corporation, 1985.

I have injected my personal prose style and grammar. Since this book combines verses from all four Gospels that relate the same narrative, verse numbers are not practical and are not used in the text. However, a complete Index of Scripture Passages provides where each verse of the four Gospels is located in this work.

The chronology that combines Matthew, Mark, Luke, and John into one narrative is my opinion based on prayerful study. The entire text is rearranged according to the time of the events. Every verse of the four Gospels is located in this book.

I made every attempt to include the points made by all four Gospel writers, on verses that cover the same subject in two or more Gospel books, and combine them into one narrative. This prevents reading, for example, a parable given by three Gospel writers three successive times.

My traditional background induced me to capitalize all references to God, Christ and the Holy Spirit—this includes personal nouns and pronouns. I do this in reverence to the Trinity.

My prayer is that God blesses this work to provide a tool for your use as directed by the Holy Spirit.

INTRODUCTION OF
THE FOUR GOSPELS

The Synoptic Gospels

A careful comparison of the four Gospels reveals that Matthew, Mark, and Luke are noticeably similar, while John is quite different. The first three Gospels agree extensively in language, in the material they include, and in the recorded order of the events and sayings from the life of Christ. As a result, these three books are called the Synoptic Gospels (*syn,* "together with"; *optic,* "seeing"; thus, "seeing together").

Author

Matthew: The early church fathers were unanimous in holding that Matthew, one of the twelve apostles, was the author of this Gospel. Matthew, whose name means "gift of the Lord," was a tax collector who left his work to follow Jesus (Matthew 9:9–13). In Mark and Luke, he is called by his other name—Levi.

Mark: Although there is no direct internal evidence of authorship, it was the unanimous testimony of the early church that this Gospel was written by John Mark. The first mention of him is in connection with his mother, who had a house in Jerusalem that served as a meeting place for believers (Acts 12:12). When Paul and Barnabas returned to Antioch from Jerusalem after the famine visit, Mark accompanied them (Acts 12:25). Mark next appears as a "helper" to Paul and Barnabas on their first missionary journey (Acts 13:5) but he deserted them at Perga, in Pamphylia, to return to Jerusalem (Acts 13:13). By the end of Paul's life, Mark had fully regained Paul's favor (see 2 Timothy 3:11).

Luke: The author's name does not appear in the book, but much unmistakable evidence points to Luke. This Gospel is a companion volume to the book of Acts; the language and structure of these two books indicate that both were written by the same person. They are addressed to the same individual, Theophilus, and the second volume refers to the first volume (Acts 1:1). Luke was probably a Gentile by birth, well educated in Greek culture, a physician by profession, a companion of Paul at various times from his second missionary journey to his first imprisonment in Rome, and a loyal friend who remained with the apostle Paul after others had deserted him (2 Timothy 4:11).

John: The author was the apostle John, "the disciple whom Jesus loved" (John 13:23; 19:26; 20:2; 21:7, 20, 24). He was prominent in the early church.

Date of Writing

Matthew: Uncertain but probably 50 to 70s.
Mark: Uncertain but probably 50 to 70.
Luke: Uncertain but probably 59 to 80s.
John: Uncertain but probably 50 to 85 or later.

Place of Writing

Matthew: Probably Palestine, though many think it may have originated in Syrian Antioch.

Mark: According to early church tradition, it was written "in the regions of Italy" or, more specifically, in Rome.

Luke: Probably Rome, though Achaia, Ephesus, and Caesarea have been suggested by some scholars.

John: Unknown but before his exile to the island of Patmos.

Recipients

Matthew: Since his Gospel was written in Greek, Matthew's readers obviously spoke Greek but they also seem to have been Jews. It has a universal outlook.

Mark: The evidence points to the church at Rome or at least to Gentile readers.

Luke: The Gospel was specifically directed to Theophilus (Luke 1:3), whose name means "one who loves God." Theophilus was possibly Luke's patron publisher, responsible for seeing that the writings were copied and distributed to believers. The message of this Gospel was also intended not only for instruction of Theophilus (Luke 1:4) but also for the instruction of those among whom the book would be circulated, both then and in the future.

John: He may have had Greek readers mainly in mind, some of whom were being exposed to heretical influence, but his primary intention was evangelistic.

Purpose

Matthew: His main purpose is to prove to his Jewish readers that Jesus is their Messiah. He does this primarily by showing how Jesus, in His life and ministry, fulfilled the Old Testament Scriptures.

Mark: Since his Gospel is traditionally associated with Rome in A.D. 64–67, it may have been occasioned by the persecutions of the Roman church. Additionally, the writing may have been to prepare his readers for this suffering by placing before them the life of our Lord.

Luke: It was written to strengthen the faith of all believers and to answer the attacks of unbelievers. It was presented to displace disconnected and ill-founded reports about Jesus. He wanted to show that the place of the Gentile Christian in God's kingdom is based on the teaching of Jesus.

John: The writer states his main purpose clearly: "These are written that you may believe that Jesus is the Christ, the Son of God and that by believing you may have life in His name" (John 20:31). Therefore, the purpose would be to build up believers as well as to win new converts.

ARRIVAL OF
THE CHRIST

Chapter 1

INTRODUCTION TO LIGHT

The Word

JOHN 1:1–18

Before time was the Word—the Word was with God and the Word was God. He was present in the beginning with God.

Through Him all things came into being—without Him nothing was made that has come into being. In Him was Life, and that Life was the Light of men. The Light shines in the darkness, but the darkness has not comprehended it and cannot put it out.

There came a man—his name was John—sent from God. His purpose was to be a witness and to testify concerning the Light so that all men might believe through him. He was not the Light but was sent to bear witness of the true Light that was coming into the world to enlighten everyone.

The Light was in the world and, even though the world was created by Him, the world did not recognize Him. He came to His own people but they rejected Him. However, for those who received Him and believed His claim, He gave the right—privilege—to become children of God, who were born neither of blood nor of a husband's will nor the decision of man but of God.

1

The Word became incarnate—flesh and blood—and lived among us. We actually saw His glory, as the only begotten Son of the Father, full of grace and truth.

John testified about Him when he cried out, saying, "This is the One of Whom I said was coming after me and that He outranks me because He existed before me." We have all received, from the abundance of His grace, blessing upon blessing. The basic law was given through Moses, but grace and truth were realized through Jesus Christ. No one has ever seen God; however, the only Son of God, Who is at the side of the Father, has declared Him—made Him known—to us.

To Theophilus

LUKE 1:1–4

Many others have undertaken to compile a narrative of the things that have been accomplished among us, just as they were of the Word. Since I have investigated all reports in close detail, starting from the story's beginning, it seemed good for me to also, most excellent Theophilus, so you can know the certain truth about what you were taught.

Chapter 2

JOHN AND JESUS

Childless Elizabeth

LUKE 1:5–25

During the days of Herod, King of Judea, there was a certain priest, named Zachariah, assigned the daily service in the division of Abijah. His wife, Elizabeth, was descended from the daughters of Aaron. Both of them lived righteously before God, careful in observing all the commandments and regulations blamelessly before God. However, they were childless because Elizabeth was barren; they were both advanced in years.

Once, while serving his priestly duty before God in the order of his division, he was chosen by lot, according to the custom of the priestly office, to enter the sanctuary of God and burn incense. When the hour to burn incense came, the assembled people were praying outside.

There appeared to him an angel of the Lord standing to the right of the altar of incense. Zachariah was paralyzed with fear when he saw him. However, the angel said to him, "Do not fear, Zachariah; your prayer has been heard. Your wife, Elizabeth, will bear a son by you, and you are to name him John. You will have joy and delight at his birth—many will rejoice because he will achieve great stature in the sight of the Lord. He will not drink wine or strong drink, and he will be filled with the Holy Spirit while yet in his mother's womb. He will turn many sons and daughters of Israel back to the Lord their God. He will go as a forerunner before the Lord, in the spirit and style of Elijah, to turn the hearts of the fathers back to the children and the disobedient to the wisdom of the righteous to make the people prepared for the Lord."

Zachariah said to the angel, "How can I believe this? I am an old man and my wife is well advanced in years."

The angel answered, "I am Gabriel and stand in the very presence of God; I was sent to bring you this good news, but because you do not believe me, you will be silent and unable to speak a word until the day of your son's birth. My words will be fulfilled in the appointed and proper time."

Meanwhile, the assembled people waiting for Zachariah were wondering what was keeping him so long in the sanctuary. When he came out, he was unable to speak; they knew he had seen a vision in the temple. He remained mute and had to use sign language with the people.

When the time of his priestly assignment was completed, he went back home. After this, his wife, Elizabeth, became pregnant and kept herself in seclusion for five months. She said, "The Lord did this for me. He looked with favor upon me and has taken away my disgrace among people."

Mary Favored

Luke 1:26–38

In the sixth month after that, God sent the angel Gabriel to Nazareth, a town in Galilee, to a virgin named Mary who was engaged to a man named Joseph, a descendant of David. Upon entering, Gabriel greeted her—he came to her—and said, "Hail, favored one! The Lord is with you."

Mary was greatly troubled at this statement and pondered what this kind of greeting meant. The angel said to her, "Mary, you have nothing to fear because you have found favor with God. You will become pregnant and give birth to a Son; you will name Him Jesus. He will be great and will be called the Son of the Most High. The Lord God will give Him the throne of His forefather David, and He will reign over the house of Jacob forever—His reign will never end."

Mary asked the angel, "How can this be since I am a virgin?"

The angel answered, "The Holy Spirit will come upon you and the power of the Most High will overshadow you. Therefore, the Holy Offspring will be called the Son of God. Behold, even your cousin Elizabeth has conceived a son in her old age—she who was said to be barren is in her sixth month. Nothing is impossible for God."

Mary said, "Behold, I am the handmaiden of the Lord. May it be done to me according to your words." Then the angel left her.

Blessed Woman

LUKE 1:39–56

Mary hastily got up and went to a town in Judah in the hill country, entered Zachariah's house, and greeted Elizabeth. When Elizabeth heard Mary's greeting, the baby leaped in her womb—Elizabeth was filled with the Holy Spirit. In a loud voice she cried out, "You are blessed among women, and blessed is the Fruit of your womb! Why am I so favored that the mother of my Lord should come to me? The moment the sound of your greeting reached my ears, the baby in my womb leaped for joy. Blessed is she who believed that there would be fulfillment of the things that the Lord spoke to her."

Mary said,

My soul glorifies the Lord,
> and my spirit rejoices in God my Savior
> because He has had regard of the humble state of His handmaiden.

From henceforth all generations will call me blessed
> because the Mighty One has done great things for me;
> Holy is His name.

His mercy is upon those who fear Him,
> from generation to generation.

He has performed mighty deeds with His arm;
> He has scattered those who are proud in the thoughts of their hearts.

He has brought down rulers from their thrones
> and exalted the humble.

He has filled the hungry with good things
> and sent the rich away empty.

He has given help to His servant Israel
> in remembrance of His mercy
> as He said to our forefathers,

to Abraham and his offspring forever.

Mary stayed with Elizabeth for about three months and then returned to her own home.

John's Birth

LUKE 1:57–80

When the time had come for Elizabeth to have her baby, she gave birth to a son. Her neighbors and relatives, when they saw that God had overwhelmed her with mercy, rejoiced with her.

On the eighth day they came to circumcise the child and were going to call him Zachariah after his father. Nevertheless, his mother said, "No. He is to be called John."

They said to her, "None of your relatives has that name."

Then they used sign language to ask Zachariah what he wanted to name the child. He asked for a tablet and, to everyone's astonishment, wrote, "His name is to be John." Immediately, his mouth was opened and his tongue was loosed—he began talking and praising God. The neighbors were filled with awe and reverential fear; all these things were talked about in all the hill country of Judea. Everyone who heard this wondered about it and asked, "What then is this child going to turn out to be?" The Lord's hand was evidently with him.

His father, Zachariah, was filled with the Holy Spirit and prophesied, saying,

Blessed be the Lord God of Israel
    because He has visited us and has redeemed His people.
He has raised up a horn of salvation for us
    in the house of David His servant,
(as He spoke through His holy prophets from ancient times).
Deliverance from our enemies
    and from the hand of all who hate us,
to show mercy to our fathers
    and to remember His holy covenant,
    the oath which He swore to Abraham our father;
to grant us that we, being delivered from the hand of our enemies,
    might enable us to serve Him without fear
    in holiness and righteousness before Him all our days.
You, my child, will be called prophet of the Most High
    because you will go before the Lord to make ready His ways,
to give the knowledge of salvation to His people
    in the forgiveness of their sins,
because of the tender mercy of God,
    by which the Rising Sun from on high will visit us
to shine upon those who sit in darkness
    and in the shadow of death,
to guide our feet into the way of peace.

The child continued to grow and to become strong in spirit. He lived in the wilderness until the day he appeared publicly in Israel.

Jesus' Genealogy

MATTHEW 1:1–17

The recorded genealogy of Jesus Christ, the Son of David, the Son of Abraham, is as follows:

Abraham fathered Isaac,
    Isaac fathered Jacob,
    Jacob fathered Judah and his brothers,
    Judah fathered Perez and Zerah, whose mother was Tamar,
    Perez fathered Hezron,
    Hezron fathered Aram (Ram),
    Aram (Ram) fathered Amminadab,
    Amminadab fathered Nahshon,
    Nahshon fathered Salmon,
    Salmon fathered Boaz, whose mother was Rahab,
    Boaz fathered Obed, whose mother was Ruth,
    Obed fathered Jesse,
    Jesse fathered King David.
David fathered Solomon, whose mother was Uriah's wife,
    Solomon fathered Rehoboam,
    Rehoboam fathered Abijah,
    Abijah fathered Asa,
    Asa fathered Jehoshaphat,
    Jehoshaphat fathered Joram (Jehoram),
    Joram (Jehoram) fathered Uzziah,
    Uzziah fathered Jotham,
    Jotham fathered Ahaz,
    Ahaz fathered Hezekiah,
    Hezekiah fathered Manasseh,
    Manasseh fathered Amon,
    Amon fathered Josiah,
    Josiah fathered Jeconiah and his brothers at the time of the deportation
        to Babylon.
After the Babylonian deportation:

Jeconiah fathered Shealtiel,
Shealtiel fathered Zerubbabel,
Zerubbabel fathered Abiud
Abiud fathered Eliakim,
Eliakim fathered Azor,
Azor fathered Zadok,
Zadok fathered Achim (Akim),
Achim (Akim) fathered Eliud,
Eliud fathered Eleazear,
Eleazear fathered Matthan,
Matthan fathered Jacob,
Jacob fathered Joseph, the husband of Mary, by whom Jesus was born,
    Who is called Christ.

Therefore, there were fourteen generations from Abraham to David, fourteen from David to the Babylonian deportation and another fourteen from the Babylonian deportation to Christ.

Jesus' Birth

MATTHEW 1:18–25
LUKE 2:1–7

The birth of Jesus Christ was as follows: His mother, Mary, was pledged to be married to Joseph but, before they were intimate, she was found to be pregnant by the Holy Spirit. Joseph, her husband, was a righteous man and, not wanting to disgrace her, decided to divorce her secretly.

As he was thinking about this, he had a dream in which an angel of the Lord said, "Joseph, son of David, do not hesitate to get married to Mary. Her pregnancy is from the Holy Spirit. She will give birth to a Son and you shall name Him Jesus" (which means Savior).

All this took place to fulfill what the Lord had spoken through the prophet: "Behold, a virgin will be pregnant with child, will give birth to a Son, and will name Him Immanuel," which means "God with us."

Then Joseph woke up; he did exactly what the angel of the Lord commanded him and took Mary to be his wife. However, he did not consummate the marriage until she gave birth to a Son—he named Him Jesus.

In those days Caesar Augustus issued a decree for a census to be taken throughout the Roman Empire—this was the first census when Quirinius was governor of Syria. Everyone had to travel to his hometown to register.

Joseph also went from the Galilean town of Nazareth to Bethlehem in Judah, David's town, for the census because he belonged to the house and family of David. He went with Mary, his fiancée, who was pregnant. While they were there, the time came for the Baby to be born—she gave birth to her firstborn Son. She wrapped Him in cloths and laid Him in a manger because there was no room for them in the inn.

Shepherds Told

LUKE 2:8–20

There were shepherds staying out in the fields watching their flocks at night. Suddenly an angel of the Lord stood among them and the glory of God shown around them—this terribly frightened them. The angel said, "Do not be afraid. I bring you good news of great joy that is meant for all people. Today a Savior has been born for you in the town of David; He is Christ, the Messiah, the Lord. This will be a sign for you to recognize Him: a Baby wrapped in cloths and lying in a manger."

Suddenly, a multitude of heavenly hosts appeared with the angel, saying,

Glory to God in the highest heaven,
peace to all men on earth with those who please Him.

When the angels withdrew into heaven, the shepherds said to each other, "Let us go and see for ourselves what the Lord has revealed to us."

They hurried off and found Mary, Joseph, and the Baby lying in the manger. When they had seen Him, they told everyone they met what the angels had said about this Child; all who heard it were astounded at what the shepherds told them. Mary kept all these things to herself and pondered them in her heart. The shepherds went back, glorifying and praising God for everything they had heard and seen, just as they had been told!

Two Blessings

LUKE 2:21–39a

When the eighth day arrived, it was time to circumcise the Baby and He was named Jesus, the name given by the angel before He was conceived in the womb.

When the days stipulated by Moses for purification were complete, they took Him up to Jerusalem to offer Him to God as commanded in the Law of the Lord, stating, "Every male who opens the womb is to be dedicated and called holy to the Lord," and also to sacrifice "a pair of doves or two pigeons," according to God's Law.

In Jerusalem at the time, there was a man named Simeon, a righteous and devout man who lived expecting the Consolation of Israel. The Holy Spirit was upon him and had shown him that he would see the Messiah before his death. Prompted by the Spirit, he entered the temple. When the parents of the Child Jesus brought Him in to carry out the custom of the Law, Simeon took Him into his arms and praised God, saying,

God, You can now release Your servant,
    as You promised.
My eyes have seen Your salvation,

which You have prepared for everyone to see:
a Light of revelation to the Gentiles
    and for the glory of Your people Israel.

Joseph and His mother marveled at these words. Simeon blessed them and said to Mary, His mother,

Behold, this Child is destined to cause the rise and fall of many in Israel
    and to be a sign that will be spoken against.
A sword will pierce through your own soul,
    revealing the secret thoughts of many hearts.

There was also a prophetess, Anna, the daughter of Phanuel of the tribe of Asher. She was very old; she had been married seven years and then lived as a widow to the age of eighty-four. She never left the temple area, worshiping night and day with fasting and prayers. At that very moment she showed up and began thanking God. She talked about the Child to all who were waiting expectantly for the deliverance of Jerusalem.

Joseph and Mary finished everything required by God in the Law.

Wise Men

MATTHEW 2:1–12

After Jesus was born in Bethlehem, Judah, during the time of King Herod, wise men arrived in Jerusalem from the East, asking, "Where can we find the newborn King of the Jews? We observed His star in the east and have come to worship Him."

When King Herod heard this he was disturbed along with all of Jerusalem. Herod gathered all the high priests and religion experts in the city together and asked them, "Where is the Christ to be born?" They replied, "Bethlehem, Judah. The prophet Micah wrote:

You, Bethlehem, in the land of Judah,
    are by no means least among the leaders of Judah;
out of you will come the Leader,
    Who will shepherd My people Israel."

Then Herod secretly called the wise men from the East and ascertained the exact time the star appeared in the sky. Then he sent them to Bethlehem and said, "Go and search carefully for the Child. As soon as you find Him, report to me so that I may go and worship Him."

Instructed by the king, they went on their way. Then the star they had seen in the east led them on until it stopped over the place of the Child. When they saw the star, they rejoiced with great joy. They entered the house and saw the Child with His mother, Mary. They fell down and worshiped Him. Then they opened their treasures and presented Him with gifts of gold, frankincense, and myrrh. Having been warned in a dream, they did not report back to Herod—they departed to their own country by another route.

To Egypt

MATTHEW 2:13–15

After the wise men were gone, an angel of the Lord appeared again to Joseph in a dream, saying, "Get up. Take the Child and His mother; flee to Egypt. Stay there until further notice, because Herod intends to hunt for this Child to kill Him."

Joseph got up and took the Child and His mother by night to Egypt and they lived there until Herod's death—this fulfilled what the Lord said through the prophet: "I called My Son out of Egypt."

Children Murdered

MATTHEW 2:16–21

Herod, when he realized that the wise men had tricked him, flew into a furious rage—he gave orders to murder all the boys in Bethlehem and its vicinity who were two years old and under according to the time that he had ascertained from the wise men. Then was fulfilled what was spoken by the prophet Jeremiah,

> A voice was heard in Ramah,
>> weeping and much mourning,
> Rachel weeping for her children
>> and she refused to be comforted
> because they were no more.

When Herod died, an angel of the Lord appeared in a dream to Joseph in Egypt, saying, "Get up. Take the Child and His mother; go to the land of Israel. Those who sought the life of the Child are dead."

Joseph got up. He took the Child and His mother to the land of Israel.

To Nazareth

MATTHEW 2:22–23
LUKE 2:39b–40

When Joseph heard that Archelaus was ruling Judea in the place of his father Herod, he was afraid to go there. Being divinely warned in a dream, he withdrew to the Galilee region and resided in the town of Nazareth. This fulfilled what was spoken through the prophets: "He shall be called a Nazarene." The Child grew and became spiritually strong. He was filled with wisdom and the grace of God was upon Him.

Father's House

LUKE 2:41–52

Every year Jesus' parents went to Jerusalem for the Feast of Passover. When He was twelve years old, they went up, as was their custom, for the Feast. When the Feast was over and they were returning home, the Boy Jesus stayed behind in Jerusalem without the knowledge of His parents. Thinking He was somewhere in their caravan, they journeyed for a day and then began looking for Him among relatives and acquaintances. When they did not find Him, they went back to Jerusalem to look for Him. After three days, they found Him in the temple sitting among the religion experts, listening to them and asking them questions. All who heard Him were amazed—they were impressed with His understanding and His answers. When His parents saw Him, they were astonished—His mother said to Him, "Son, why have You done this to us? Your father and I have been distressed and anxiously looking for You."

He said, "Why were you looking for Me? Did you not know that it was necessary for Me to be in My Father's house?" They did not comprehend what He was saying to them.

He went back to Nazareth with them and continued to be obedient to them. His mother treasured all these things deep within herself. Jesus kept increasing in wisdom and stature; He was in the favor of God and men.

Chapter 3

JESUS IS INTRODUCED

John's Preaching

MATTHEW 3:1–12
MARK 1:1–8
LUKE 3:1–18
JOHN 1:19–28

In the fifteenth year of the rule of Tiberius Caesar—when Pontius Pilate was governor of Judea; when Herod was tetrarch of Galilee and his brother Philip was tetrarch of Iturea and Trachonitis; when lysanias was tetrarch of Abilene—during the high priesthood of Annas and Caiaphas, John (called "the Baptizer"), the son of Zachariah, received a message from God while he was in the wilderness. He went into all the area around the Jordan River preaching a baptism of repentance for the forgiveness of sins. His message was plain and simple like his wilderness surroundings: "Change your life because God's kingdom is here."

The good news—the Gospel—of Jesus Christ begins here. John and his preaching, following the words from the scroll of the prophet Isaiah, were authorized by Isaiah's prophecy:

I am sending My preacher ahead of You;
    He will make the road smooth for You.
Thunder in the desert!
Prepare for God's arrival!
    Make the road smooth and straight!
Every valley will be filled in,
    every mountain and hill smoothed out.
The detours will be straightened out,
    all the rough roads smoothed over.
Everyone will see God's salvation.

John appeared in the wild, dressed in camel's hair clothing that was tied at the waist by a leather belt. He preached a baptism of repentance that leads to forgiveness of sins. He lived on a diet of locusts and wild field honey. People went out to him from Jerusalem, Judea, and the region of the Jordan River to hear and see him preach. There at the Jordan River, those who came to confess their sins were baptized by him.

When John realized that crowds, including many Pharisees and Sadducees, were showing up where he was baptizing because it was becoming the popular thing to do, he exploded, saying, "You brood of snakes! What do you think you are doing slithering down to this river? Do you think water on your skin is going to make any difference and deflect God's judgment? Your life is what must change, not your skin! Do not presume to think you can say of yourselves, 'Abraham is our father.' Being a descendant of Abraham is not important. God can make descendants for Abraham from stones. What counts is whether or not your life is fruitful. Is it green and blossoming? If it is deadwood, it goes into the fire."

The crowd asked him, "What shall we do, then?"

John replied, "If you have two coats, give one away and do the same with your food."

Tax collectors also came to be baptized and asked, "Teacher, what should we do, then?"

He told them, "Collect no more than what is required by law."

Some soldiers questioned him, asking, "What should we do, then?"

He answered, "No shakedowns, no blackmail, and be content with your wages."

The people were waiting expectantly and wondering in their hearts whether John might be the Christ.

John answered them by saying, "I baptize you with water to turn your old life in for a new life for God. However, He who is mightier than I is coming, the strap of Whose sandals I am not fit to unfasten. He will baptize you with the Holy Spirit and with fire. He is going to clean the house of your lives. He will place everything true in its proper place before God and everything false He will put out to be burned with the trash."

This is what John preached when Jews from Jerusalem sent priests and Levites to ask him, "Who are you?" He was completely honest, did not evade the question, and freely admitted the truth, saying, "I am not the Christ!"

They asked him, "Who are you, then? Are you Elijah?"

He replied, "I am not."

Then they asked him, "Are you the Prophet?"

He answered, "No!"

Finally they inquired, "Who are you, then? We need an answer for those who sent us. Tell us something; what do you say about yourself?"

John replied in the words of Isaiah the prophet: "I am the voice of one shouting in the wilderness, 'Make straight the way of the Lord.'"

Those sent to question him were from the Pharisees, who now asked, "If you are neither the Christ nor Elijah nor the Prophet, why do you baptize?"

John replied, "I only baptize using water. A Person you do not recognize stands in your midst. He comes after me, but He is not in second place to me. I am not even worthy to hold His coat for Him."

These things happened in Bethany on the other side of the Jordan River, where John was baptizing at the time.

With many other words John exhorted the people and preached the good news—the Gospel—to them.

Jesus Baptized

MATTHEW 3:13–17
MARK 1:9–11
LUKE 3:21–22
JOHN 1:29–34

The next day, when all the people were being baptized, John saw Jesus coming toward him at the Jordan River from Nazareth in Galilee and exclaimed, "Behold, the Lamb of God, Who takes away the sin of the world! This is the One I meant when I said I did not know Who He was, but He is the reason I came baptizing in water—so He might be revealed to Israel." He wanted John to baptize Him but John objected, saying, "I am the one who needs to be baptized, not You!"

However, Jesus insisted, saying, "Permit it now to fulfill all righteousness." John then consented to baptize Him.

The moment Jesus came up out of the water—He was praying—the skies opened up and He saw God's Spirit—it looked like a dove—descending and landing on Him. A voice from heaven said, "This is My Son Whom I love; I am well pleased with Him."

John gave this further testimony, saying, "I watched the Spirit, like a dove, come down from the sky and remain upon Him. Again I state that I know nothing about Him except that the One Who authorized me to baptize with water told me, 'The One on Whom you see the Spirit come down and stay, this One will baptize with the Holy Spirit.' That is exactly what I saw happen, and I am telling you that He is the Son of God."

Joseph's Ancestry

LUKE 3:23–38

Jesus began His ministry when He was about thirty years old. He was thought to be the son of Joseph,

son of Heli (Eli),
son of Matthat,
son of Levi,
son of Melchi (Melki),
son of Jannai,
son of Joseph,
son of Mattathias,
son of Amos,
son of Nahum,
son of Elsi (Hesli),
son of Naggai,
son of Maath,
son of Mattathias,
son of Semein,
son of Josech,
son of Joda,
son of Joanan,
son of Rhesa,
son of Zerubbabel,
son of Shealtiel,
son of Neri,
son of Melchi (Melki),
son of Addi,
son of Cosam,
son of Elmadam,
son of Er,
son of Joshua,
son of Eliezer,
son of Jorim,

son of Matthat,
son of Levi,
son of Simeon,
son of Judah,
son of Joseph,
son of Jonam,
son of Eliakim,
son of Melea,
son of Menna,
son of Mattatha,
son of Nathan,
son of David,
son of Jesse,
son of Obed,
son of Boaz,
son of Salmon (Sala),
son of Nahshon,
son of Amminadab,
son of Ram (Aram),
son of Admin,
son of Arni,
son of Hezron,
son of Perez,
son of Judah,
son of Jacob,
son of Isaac,
son of Abraham,
son of Terah,
son of Nahor,
son of Serug,
son of Reu,
son of Peleg,
son of Eber (Haber),
son of Shelah,
son of Cainan,

son of Arphaxad,

son of Shem,

son of Noah,

son of Lamech,

son of Methuselah,

son of Enoch,

son of Jared,

son of Mahalaleel (Mahalalel),

son of Cainan (Kenan),

son of Enos (Enosh),

son of Seth,

son of Adam,

son of God.

Jesus Tempted

MATTHEW 4:1–11
MARK 1:12–13
LUKE 4:1–13

Then Jesus, full of the Holy Spirit, immediately left the Jordan and was led by the Spirit into the wilderness to be tested by the devil for forty days. During this time wild animals were His companions and He ate nothing during those days—He was hungry.

Then the devil said to Him, "If You are God's Son, order this stone to become a loaf of bread."

Jesus answered, "It is written that man shall not live only on bread but by every word of God."

For another test the devil took Him to Jerusalem. He put Him on top of the temple and said, "If You are God's Son, jump down from here. It is written: 'He has charged His angels to protect You. They will catch You so that You will not strike Your foot on a stone.'"

Jesus answered, "The Scripture says not to test the Lord your God."

For still another test, the devil took Him to a high mountain and showed Him all the kingdoms of the earth in a moment of time and said to Him, "I will give You all of this domain and its glory—it has been handed over to me and I can give it to anyone I desire. Therefore, if You worship me it shall all be Yours."

Jesus answered, "Go away, Satan. It is written: 'Worship only the Lord your God, and Him alone shall you serve.'"

The devil left Him when he finished all this tempting, but only temporarily until another more opportune time. Then angels came and ministered to His needs.

Chapter 4

JESUS' EARLY MINISTRY

Messiah Found

JOHN 1:35–51

The next day John was standing with two disciples. He looked at Jesus walking nearby and said, "Behold, the Lamb of God!"

When the two disciples heard him say this, they followed Jesus. As He turned and saw them, He asked, "What do you seek?"

They said, "Rabbi" (which means Teacher), "where are You staying?"

Jesus replied, "Come along and see for yourselves."

They came, saw where He was living, and spent the day with Him. This happened about the tenth hour—about four o'clock.

Andrew, Simon Peter's brother, was one of the two who heard what John said and followed Jesus. The first thing he did after finding where Jesus lived was find his brother, Simon, telling him, "We have found the Messiah" (that is, the Christ). He immediately brought him to Jesus.

Jesus looked at him and said, "You are John's son, Simon. You shall be called Cephas"—Peter when translated—which means a stone or rock.

The next day, Jesus decided to go into Galilee. He found Philip and said to him, "Come, follow Me."

Philip's hometown was Bethsaida, the same as Andrew and Peter. Philip found Nathanael and told him, "We have found the One Moses wrote about in the law, the One written about by the prophets. It is Jesus of Nazareth, the Son of Joseph."

Nathanael asked, "Can any good thing come out of Nazareth?"

Philip said, "Come and see for yourself."

When Jesus saw Nathanael coming, He said, "Behold, a real Israelite in whom there is nothing false."

Nathanael asked, "How do You know these things about me?"

Jesus answered, "One day, long before Philip called you here, I saw you under the fig tree."

Nathanael declared, "Rabbi! You are the Son of God; You are the King of Israel!"

Jesus said, "You have become a believer simply because I told you I saw you one day sitting under the fig tree? You shall see greater things than these." Jesus added, "I tell you the truth, you shall see heaven open and God's angels ascending and descending upon the Son of Man."

Wedding Wine

JOHN 2:1–12

Three days later there was a wedding at Cana in Galilee. Jesus' mother was there. Jesus and His disciples had also been invited to the wedding. When the wine was gone, Jesus' mother said to Him, "They have no more wine."

Jesus replied, "Dear woman, why do you involve Me? My time to act has not yet come."

His mother told the servants, "Whatever He tells you, do it."

Six stoneware water jars were there, the kind used by the Jews for ceremonial washings. Each held two or three firkins—twenty to thirty gallons. Jesus said to the servants, "Fill the jars with water." They filled them to the brim.

Then He told them, "Now fill your pitchers and take them to the host." They did as He instructed them.

When the master of the banquet tasted the water that had become wine—he did not know what had just happened even though the servants knew—he called the bridegroom and said, "Everybody I know begins with their finest wines and, after the guests have had their fill, brings in the cheaper wine; however, you have saved the best until now!"

This act in Cana of Galilee was the first miracle Jesus performed, the first glimpse of His glory, and His disciples believed in Him.

After this He went down to Capernaum along with His mother, brothers, and disciples. There they stayed a few days.

Jesus' Authority

JOHN 2:13–25

When the Jewish Feast of Passover was about to take place, Jesus went up to Jerusalem. He found in the temple enclosure an abundance of people selling cattle, sheep, and doves, along with those sitting at their stands changing money.

Jesus made a whip out of cords and drove them all out of the temple, along with the sheep and cattle. He scattered the money changers' coins and overturned their tables. He said to those selling doves, "Get your things out of here! Stop making My Father's house into a marketplace!" That is when His disciples remembered that it is written, "Zeal for Your house will consume Me."

Then the Jews retorted, "What miracle can You give us as evidence of Your authority to do these things?"

Jesus answered, "Tear down this temple, and in three days I will raise it again."

The Jews replied, "It took forty-six years to build this temple, and You are going to raise it in three days?" However, He was referring to

His body as the temple. After He was raised from the dead, His disciples remembered what He had said at this time. They then believed what was written in Scripture and what Jesus had said to the Jews.

When He was in Jerusalem at the Feast of Passover, many people saw the miracles He was doing and believed in His name. However, Jesus did not trust Himself to them because He knew all men—He did not need a testimony about man from men because He knew human nature.

Born Again

JOHN 3:1–21

There was a man of the Pharisees named Nicodemus who was a leader among the Jews. He came to Jesus and said, "Rabbi, we are certain You are a Teacher from God because no one could perform all these miracles unless God was with him."

Jesus answered, "I assure you that unless a person is born from above, it is not possible to see the kingdom of God."

Nicodemus asked, "How can anyone be born when he is grown up and old? He cannot re-enter his mother's womb and be born again."

Jesus said, "I tell you the truth, unless a man is born of water and the Spirit, he can never enter the kingdom of God. What is born from flesh is flesh, and what is born of the Spirit is spirit. You should not marvel at My saying, 'You must be born again.' The wind blows wherever it pleases and, although you hear its sound, you neither know where it comes from nor where it goes. This is the way it is with everyone born of the Spirit."

Nicodemus asked, "How can this be possible?"

Jesus answered, "You are a teacher of Israel and you do not understand these things? I tell you the truth, We speak only of what We know and We testify only to what We have seen with Our own eyes, but you still do not accept Our testimony. I have told you of things on earth and you do not believe. How can you believe if I speak of heavenly things? No one has ever ascended into heaven except the One Who descended from heaven—the Son of Man. Just as Moses lifted the serpent in the desert, even so the Son of Man must be lifted up so that whoever believes in Him will have eternal life.

"This is how much God loved the world: He gave His one and only Son so that whoever believes in Him shall not perish but have everlasting life. God did not send His Son into the world to condemn it but so the world might find salvation through Him. Those who believe in Him are not condemned, but those who do not believe in the Son of God are condemned already. This is the verdict: the Light has come into the world, but men loved the darkness instead of the Light because they were evil. All wrongdoers hate the Light and avoid the Light because it exposes their deeds. On the other hand, whoever practices truth comes into the Light so that his deeds are plainly shown for what he has done through God."

More Prominent

JOHN 3:22–36

After this, Jesus and His disciples went into the Judean countryside, where He spent some time with them and baptized believers. John was also baptizing at Aenon near Salim where water was abundant—people constantly came to be baptized by him. This was before John was thrown into jail. John's disciples got into an argument with a Jew about ceremonial washing. They came to John and said, "Rabbi, the One Who was with you on the other side of the Jordan River—the One you testified about—He is also baptizing and everyone is going to Him."

John answered, "A man can receive nothing unless it is given to him from heaven. You yourselves were there when I publicly said, 'I am not the Messiah but was sent ahead of Him to get things ready.' He who has the bride is the bridegroom, but the friend of the bridegroom stands by and listens for him, rejoicing when he hears the bridegroom's voice. This then is my joy and it is now complete. He must become more prominent and I must become less prominent.

"The One Who comes from heaven is above all others, while he who is of the earth is from the earth and speaks of the earth. He testifies to what He has actually seen and heard, but no one accepts His witness. Whoever accepts His testimony certifies that God is truth. The One that God sent speaks the words of God—God gives the Spirit without measure. The Father loves the Son and has entrusted all things into His hands. Those who believe in the Son have eternal life, but those who do not obey and reject the Son will not see life because God's wrath remains on them."

Living Water

JOHN 4:1–30

When Jesus realized that the Pharisees had heard that He was gaining and baptizing more disciples than John (although His disciples, not Jesus, did the actual baptizing), He left Judea and returned to Galilee.

To get there, it was necessary for Him to pass through Samaria. He came into Sychar, a Samaritan town that bordered the parcel of land Jacob had given his son Joseph—Jacob's well was still there. Jesus, tired from the journey, sat down at the well. It was about the sixth hour—noon.

When a Samaritan woman came to draw water, Jesus said to her, "Would you give Me a drink?" (His disciples had gone to the town to buy food.)

The Samaritan woman said to Him, "How come You, a Jew, are asking me, a Samaritan woman, for a drink?" (Jews do not associate with Samaritans.)

Jesus answered her, "If you knew the generosity of God and Who it is that asks you for a drink, you would be asking Me for a drink and I would give you living water."

The woman said, "Sir, You do not have anything to draw with and the well is deep. How are You going to get this living water? Are You greater than our ancestor Jacob who gave us this well and drank from it himself, along with his sons and livestock?"

Jesus answered her, "Everyone who drinks this water will get thirsty again, but anyone who drinks the water I give will never thirst again. The water I give will become a spring of water flowing continually within him to eternal life."

The woman said to Him, "Sir, give me this water so I will never get thirsty and will never have to come back to this well again to draw water!"

Jesus said to her, "Go call your husband and then come back."

"I have no husband," she replied to Him.

Jesus said to her, "You are right when you say, 'I have no husband,' because you have had five husbands, and the man you live with is not your husband. You have spoken the truth."

The woman said to Him, "Sir, I perceive that You are a prophet. Our ancestors worshiped God at this mountain, but you Jews insist that Jerusalem is the place we ought to worship."

Jesus said to her, "A time is coming when you will worship the Father neither here at this mountain nor there in Jerusalem. You Samaritans worship what you do not comprehend; we Jews worship what we have knowledge of and understand. A time is coming, and has now come, when genuine worshipers will worship the Father in spirit and truth—such are the kind of worshipers the Father seeks. God is spirit, and those who worship Him must worship in spirit and truth."

The woman said, "I do know that the Messiah is coming one day. When He arrives, He will make everything clear to us."

Jesus said, "I Who speak to you now am He."

Just then His disciples returned and were surprised to find Him talking to a woman, but no one asked, "What do you want?" or "Why do You speak to Her?"

Then the woman left her jar, went back to the town, and told the people, "Come and see a Man Who knew all the things I ever did in my life. Do you think this could be the Messiah?" The people went out of the town to go to Him.

Ripe Fields

JOHN 4:31–42

In the meantime, the disciples urged Him, saying, "Rabbi, eat something."

However, He told them, "I have food to eat that you know nothing about."

The disciples said to each other, "Has someone brought Him food?"

Jesus said, "My food is to do the will of the One Who sent Me and to complete His work. Do you not say, 'In about four months it will be time to harvest?' Behold, I tell you to open your eyes and observe the fields that are ripe for harvest. Already the reaper is getting his wages and is gathering the fruit for eternal life so that the one who sows and the one who reaps rejoice together—the saying 'One sows and another reaps' is true. I sent you to reap a crop for which you did not work. Others have labored and you step in to reap the benefit of their work."

Many of the Samaritans from that town believed in Him because of the woman's witness: "He knew all about the things I ever did in my life." When the Samaritans arrived, they asked Him to stay with them and He stayed two days. A lot more people believed because of what He had to say.

They said to the woman, "We no longer believe just because of what you told us. We have heard it for ourselves and know that this Man is the Savior of the world."

Galilean Prophet

JOHN 4:43–45

After the two days, He left for Galilee. Jesus Himself declared that a prophet is not respected in the place where he grew up. Consequently, when He arrived in Galilee, the Galileans welcomed Him only because they had seen all the things He had done in Jerusalem during the Feast of Passover—they had also been to the feast.

Prophetic Words

MATTHEW 4:12–22
MARK 1:14–20
LUKE 4:14–30

After John was put in prison, Jesus got word that he had been arrested, and He returned to Galilee in the power of the Spirit, preaching the good news of God, saying, "The appointed time has come—God's kingdom is here. Repent and believe the good news." Word that He was back spread throughout the countryside. He taught in their synagogues and everyone praised Him.

He came to Nazareth where He had been brought up and, as was His custom on the Sabbath, He went to the synagogue. When He stood up to read, He was handed the scroll of the prophet Isaiah. He unrolled the scroll and found the place where it was written:

The Spirit of the Lord is on Me,
　　He has anointed Me to preach the good news to the poor,
He has sent Me to proclaim pardon to prisoners
　　and recovery of sight to the blind,
to set free those who are oppressed,
　　to proclaim the acceptable year of the Lord.

Then He rolled up the scroll, gave it back to the assistant and sat down. The eyes of everyone in the synagogue were gazing on Him and He began to say to them, "Today this scripture has been fulfilled in your hearing."

All spoke well of Him and marveled at the gracious words that came from His mouth. They asked, "Is this not Joseph's Son, the One we have known since He was a youngster?"

Jesus answered them, "Doubtless you are going to quote the proverb, 'Physician, heal Yourself.' Do here in Your hometown what we heard You did in Capernaum." He continued, "I tell you the truth, no prophet is accepted in his hometown. In truth I tell you that there were many widows in Israel at the time of Elijah, during the three and a half years of drought, when a severe famine devastated the land. However, Elijah was not sent to any of them except to Zarephath" (Sarepta), "in the land of Sidon. Also, there were many lepers in Israel during the time of the prophet Elisha, but none of them were cleansed except Naaman the Syrian."

That made everyone in the synagogue furious. They got up and drove Him out of the town—took Him to the mountain cliff at the edge of the town to throw Him down. Nevertheless, He passed through the midst of them and went on His way.

Leaving His hometown Nazareth, He went to live in Capernaum by the sea in the region of Zebulun and Naphtali to fulfill what was spoken through the prophet Isaiah:

Land of Zebulun and land of Naphtali,
 the way to the sea, beyond the Jordan River,
  Galilee of the Gentiles;
the people living in the dark
 saw a great Light;
for those who were living in the land and shadow of death,
 a Light has dawned upon them.

From that time on Jesus began to preach, saying, "Repent, for the kingdom of heaven is at hand."

As He walked by the Sea of Galilee, Jesus saw two brothers: Simon, who was called Peter, and his brother Andrew. They were casting a net into the lake—they were fishermen. Jesus said to them, "Come follow Me and I will make you fishers of men." They immediately left their nets and followed Him.

Going on a little further, He saw and came upon another pair of brothers, James and John, Zebedee's sons. These two were sitting in a boat with their father, Zebedee, mending their nets. Immediately, Jesus made the same offer to them, and they were just as quick to follow Him—they abandoned the boat, their father, Zebedee, and the hired hands.

Authoritative Teaching

MARK 1:21–28
LUKE 4:31–37

Then they went to Capernaum, a town in Galilee. When the Sabbath arrived, Jesus immediately went to the synagogue and began to teach. The people were amazed at His teaching; His message had authority—not like the religion experts. Suddenly, there was a man in their synagogue who was possessed by a demon. He cried out, "Ha! What business do You have here with us, Jesus of Nazareth? Have You come to destroy us? I know Who You are—the Holy One of God!"

Jesus rebuked him, saying, "Be quiet and come out of him!" The demon threw the man down in convulsions in their midst and came out of the man without injuring him.

All the people were amazed and asked each other, "What kind of teaching is this? His words have authority. He gives orders to demons and they obey Him—they come out!" News about Him quickly spread over the entire region of Galilee.

All Healed

MATTHEW 8:14–17
MARK 1:29–34
LUKE 4:38–41

Jesus left the synagogue and went with James and John to the house of Simon Peter. On entering, Jesus was told about and found Simon Peter's mother-in-law sick in bed, burning up with a high fever, and they asked

Him to help her. He went to her, stood over her, took her hand, told the fever to leave, and raised her up. The fever was gone—it left. Immediately, when the fever left her, she got up and began to wait on them.

That evening, after the sun was down, the people brought to Jesus those who were sick and those possessed by a demon—the whole town gathered at His door. He drove out the demons—they came out of people, screaming, "You are the Son of God!" However, He shut them up, refusing to let them speak because they knew Him to be the Messiah; because the demons knew His true identity, He did not let them say a word. He cured the sick—one by one He placed His hands on them and healed them. This fulfilled what was spoken through the prophet Isaiah:

> He took our illnesses
> and carried away our diseases.

Other Towns

MATTHEW 4:23–25
MARK 1:35–39
LUKE 4:42–44

Early in the morning, at daybreak when it was still dark, Jesus got up and went out to a secluded spot to pray. Simon and the people with him went looking for Him. When they found Him, they exclaimed, "Everybody is looking for You!"

Jesus said, "Let us go to other towns so I can preach there also. This is why I have come." He left the next day for other regions. The crowds looked for Him and, when they found Him, clung to Him so He could not continue. He told them, "Do you not realize that there are yet other towns where I have to tell the good news of God's kingdom—that this is the work God sent Me to do?"

Meanwhile, from there He went to Galilee and continued preaching—He went to their synagogues throughout Galilee, preaching the truth and casting out demons. God's kingdom was His theme—He taught that beginning right now they were under God's good government. He also healed people of their diseases and of the results of their bad lives. The report of Him spread throughout Syria—people brought anybody with an ailment, whether mental, emotional, or physical, and Jesus healed them all. Crowds came not only from Galilee but also from Decapolis, Jerusalem, Judea, and from across the Jordan River.

Catching Men

LUKE 5:1–11

One day, as Jesus was standing on the shore of Lake Gennesaret and the people pressed in on Him to hear the Word of God, He noticed two boats at the water's edge. The fishermen had just left them and were out cleaning their nets. He climbed into the boat that belonged to Simon Peter and asked him to put out a little from the shore. He sat down and taught the people from the boat.

When He finished teaching, He said to Simon, "Push out into deep water and let down your nets for a catch."

Simon said, "Master, we have been fishing hard all night and caught nothing. In spite of this, because You say so, I will let down the nets."

As soon as they did so, they caught such a great quantity of fish that their nets began to break. They signaled to their partners in the other boat to come and help them—they came and filled both boats so much that they began to sink.

When Simon Peter saw this, he fell at the knees of Jesus and said, "Master, depart from me because I am a sinful man, O Lord!" He said this because he and his partners were astonished at the large catch of fish. It was the same with James and John, Zebedee's sons, coworkers with Simon.

Then Jesus said to Simon, "There is nothing to fear. From now on you will be catching men." They pulled their boats up on the shore, left everything, and followed Him.

Leper Healed

MATTHEW 8:1–4
MARK 1:40–45
LUKE 5:12–16

When Jesus came down the mountain, large crowds followed Him. While He was in one of the towns, a man came covered with leprosy. The leper appeared, saw Jesus, came to Him, and went to his knees—he fell down and begged, "Master, if You want to, You can heal my body and make me clean."

Moved with compassion, Jesus reached out His hand and touched him, saying, "I want to; be clean!" Immediately, all signs of the leprosy were gone and he was cured—his, skin was smooth and healthy. Jesus then ordered him and instructed him, saying, "Do not tell anyone about this. Take the offering for cleansing that Moses ordered and prescribed for your healing. Present your healed body to the priest, along with the appropriate offering of thanks to God and as evidence to the people." However, the man did not keep it to himself and the word spread. As soon as the man departed, he told everyone he met what had happened, spreading the news all over town. Soon a large crowd of people had gathered to listen and be healed of their sicknesses. Whenever possible, Jesus withdrew for prayer to secluded places because He was no longer able to move freely in and out of the towns—people found Him and came from everywhere.

Paralytic Healed

MATTHEW 9:1–8
MARK 2:1–12
LUKE 5:17–26

A few days later, Jesus got into a boat and crossed the sea with His disciples to His hometown, Capernaum. Word spread that He was back home. They were hardly out of the boat when a crowd gathered and clogged the entrance to the house so no one could get in or out—He was teaching the Word. As He taught, Pharisees and religion experts were sitting around—they had come from every town in Galilee, Judea, and Jerusalem.

Four men carried a paralytic on a stretcher, looking for a way to get into the house and set him before Jesus. When they were not able to enter because of the crowd, they went up on the roof, removed some of the tiles, and lowered the paralytic on his stretcher in the middle of the crowd in front of Him. Jesus was impressed by their faith and said to the paralytic, "Friend, your sins are forgiven." That caused the Pharisees and religion experts who were sitting there to think and whisper among themselves, "Why does He speak this way? That is blasphemy! Only God can forgive sins."

Jesus became immediately aware in His spirit what they were thinking and said, "Why are you thinking these things? Which do you think is easier, to say to the paralytic, 'I forgive your sins,' or to say, 'Get up, take your stretcher, and start walking'? So that you know that the Son of Man is authorized to do either or both ..." (At this He turned to, looked at, and spoke directly to the paralytic) "... arise, pick up your bed-mat, and go home." Immediately, the man got up, took his blanket, grabbed his bed mat, walked out, and departed for home, praising God all the way in view of them all. Everyone was amazed and they praised God, saying, "We have never seen anything like this—we have seen remarkable things today!" The crowd was awestruck, amazed and pleased that God had authorized Jesus to work among them this way.

Doctor Needed

MATTHEW 9:9–13
MARK 2:13–17
LUKE 5:27–32

Once again, Jesus went out to walk beside the lake. A large crowd came to Him and He began to teach them. Walking along, He saw a man named Levi (Matthew), son of Alphaeus, at his work collecting taxes. Jesus said, "Come with Me." Matthew did—he stood up, walked away from everything, and followed Him.

While Jesus was having dinner at Levi's house with His close followers (disciples), a large crowd was there—tax collectors and a lot of disreputable people came and joined them as guests at the dinner. Many religion experts and Pharisees saw Him eating with this kind of people. They complained to His disciples, greatly offended, and asked them, "Why does He eat with tax collectors and disreputable people?"

Jesus, on hearing this, answered them, saying, "Who needs a doctor, the healthy or the sick? Go and learn what this means: 'I desire mercy and not religious sacrifices.' The sick need a doctor, not the healthy. I have come to call sinners to repentance, not the righteous."

Fasting Time

MATTHEW 9:14–17
MARK 2:18–22
LUKE 5:33–39

The disciples of John and the disciples of the Pharisees observed the practice of fasting. Some people—John's followers—approached a little later and asked Jesus, "Why is it that we and the Pharisees fast often but Your disciples do not fast? Your disciples continue to eat and drink. Why?"

Jesus answered them, saying, "When you celebrate a wedding, guests of the bridegroom do not fast while he is with them. When the bridegroom is gone, on that day they will fast."

Jesus continued with a parable, saying, "No one tears a patch of cloth that has not been shrunk from a new garment and sews it on an old fabric—it will make the tear worse. Also, you do not put your wine into old wineskins because the wine will run out, and both the wine and wineskins will be ruined—new wine is poured into new wineskins to preserve both. Additionally, no one who tastes aged wine prefers new wine, because he says, 'The aged wine is better.'"

Sabbath Intent

MATTHEW 12:1–14
MARK 2:23–3:6
LUKE 6:1–11

One Sabbath Jesus was walking with His disciples through a field of grain. As His disciples walked along, they were picking off some heads of grain, rubbing them in their hands to get rid of the chaff, and eating the kernels. Some Pharisees asked Jesus, "Why are Your disciples doing what is unlawful on the Sabbath?"

Jesus answered them, saying, "Have you ever read what David and his companions did when they were hungry? In the days when Abiathar was high priest, he entered the house of God and ate the consecrated bread, which, according to law, no one but priests were allowed to eat. He also gave some to his companions. Did you ever read the law that priests carrying out their temple duties break Sabbath rules, desecrate the day, and yet are innocent? I say to you that One greater than the temple is here. If you had only known the meaning of the saying 'I prefer compassionate mercy rather than religious sacrifice,' you would not have condemned the innocent. The Sabbath was made to serve man and not for man to serve the Sabbath. The Son of Man is Lord of the Sabbath."

Jesus left the field and, on another Sabbath, He went back to the synagogue and taught. There was a man there with a withered right hand. The religion experts and Pharisees watched Jesus to see if He would heal the man, hoping for a reason to accuse Him of a Sabbath infraction by healing on that day. They said to Jesus, "Is it legal to heal on the Sabbath?"

Jesus knew what they were thinking and spoke to the man with the withered hand, saying, "Get up and stand here in the midst of us." The man arose and did as Jesus told him.

Then Jesus said, "I ask you, is it lawful and right on the Sabbath to do good or to do harm, to save a life or destroy it? Is there a person here who, finding one of your sheep fallen into a pit, would not grab it and lift it out, even though it was the Sabbath? Man is more valuable than a sheep; for that reason, it is lawful to do good on the Sabbath."

Jesus looked around at all of them and said to the man, "Hold out your hand." The man held it out and it was completely healed—it was like new. The Pharisees walked out, furious, and plotted with each other what they might do to kill Jesus.

Twelve Apostles

MATTHEW 12:15–21
MARK 3:7–19
LUKE 6:12–19

Being aware of this, Jesus withdrew with His disciples to the lake. However, a lot of people followed Him—a large crowd from Galilee followed them, along with many people from Judea, Jerusalem, Idumea, across the Jordan River, and around Tyre and Sidon (many people who had heard the reports and had come to see for themselves). He told His disciples to get a boat ready so He would not be crushed by the crowd. He healed many people; everyone who had any ailment was pushing forward to get near and touch Him. He healed them all. He also cautioned them not to make Him publicly known. This was in fulfillment of what was spoken through the prophet Isaiah:

> Behold, here is My chosen Servant,
>   the One I love and with Whom I delight;
> I will place My Spirit upon Him,
>   and He will proclaim justice to the nations.
> He will not quarrel or raise His voice,
>   nor will anyone hear His voice in the streets.

A bruised reed He will not break,
>   and a dimly burning wick He will not put out
>   until He brings victory to justice and a just cause.
On His name will the Gentiles put their hope.

Whenever the demons recognized Him, they fell down before Him and cried out, "You are the Son of God!" However, He shut them up by warning them not to make Him known publicly.

At about that same time, Jesus went to a mountain to pray—He spent the entire night praying to God. When morning came, He summoned His disciples to Him and selected twelve of them, whom He designated apostles. These are the twelve:

Simon (Jesus later named him Peter, meaning "Rock"),
Andrew, his brother,
James, son of Zebedee,
John, brother of James (Jesus nicknamed the Zebedee brothers
    Boanerges, meaning "Sons of Thunder"),
Philip,
Bartholomew,
Matthew,
Thomas,
James, son of Alphaeus,
Thaddaeus, son of James (also known as Judas),
Simon the Canaanite (called the Zealot), and
Judas Iscariot (who betrayed Him).

He descended the mountain with them and stood on a level spot surrounded by disciples. A great number of people from all over Judea, Jerusalem, and the coastal towns of Tyre and Sidon had come both to hear Him and to be cured of their ailments. Those disturbed by demons were healed by Him. The multitude tried to touch Him because power was coming from Him, healing all of them.

The Blessed

MATTHEW 5:1–12
LUKE 6:20–26

When Jesus saw the crowds, He went up on a mountainside and sat down. Then His disciples came to Him. He looked at them and began to teach them, saying,

Blessed are the poor in spirit and those who are poor, because theirs is the kingdom of heaven—theirs is the kingdom of God.

Blessed are those who mourn, because they will receive comfort.

Blessed are the gentle and patient, because they will inherit the earth.

Blessed are those who hunger and thirst now for righteousness, because they will be completely satisfied.

Blessed are the merciful, because they shall receive mercy.

Blessed are those who weep now, because they will laugh.

Blessed are the pure in heart, because they will see God.

Blessed are the peacemakers, because they will be called sons of God.

Blessed are those who are persecuted for the sake of righteousness, because theirs is the kingdom of heaven.

Blessed are you when men hate you, persecute you, falsely say all kinds of evil against you because of Me, ostracize you, cast insults at you, and defame your name on account of the Son of Man. Be glad and leap for joy in that day, because great is your reward in heaven—that is how their fathers mistreated the prophets who were before you.

Jesus continued, saying, "However, it is trouble ahead for those who are rich, because you are already receiving your reward. It is trouble for those who are well fed now, because you will be hungry. It is trouble for those who laugh now, because you will mourn and weep. It is trouble for those who men speak of well, because their forefathers treated the false prophets the same way."

You Are

MATTHEW 5:13–16

Jesus continued, saying, "You are here to be the salt of the earth. However, if salt has lost its saltiness, how can it again be salty? It is no longer good for anything except to be thrown out and trampled underfoot by men.

"You are the light of the world. You cannot hide a city that sits on a hill. Nor do people light a lamp and then put it under a bowl—they put it on a lamp stand and it gives light to everyone in the house. Likewise, let your light shine before men so they can see your good works and praise your Father in heaven."

God's Law

MATTHEW 5:17–20

Jesus continued, saying, "Do not think that I have come to do away with the law or the prophets—I am not here to abolish them but to complete them. I tell you the truth, until sky and earth pass away, neither the smallest letter nor the least stroke of the pen will disappear from the law until the accomplishment of all things.

"Whoever breaks even the least of these commandments and teaches others to do the same will be called least important in the kingdom of heaven, but whoever practices and teaches these commands will be called great in the kingdom of heaven. I tell you the truth, unless your righteousness surpasses and is more than that of the religion experts and the Pharisees, you will not enter the kingdom of heaven."

Murder Judgment

MATTHEW 5:21–26

Jesus continued, saying, "You have heard what was said to the people long ago, 'Do not murder' and, 'Whoever murders will be subject to judgment by the court.' However, I say to you that anyone who continues to be angry with his brother is subject to the court's judgment. Whoever speaks insultingly to his brother is guilty before the court. Whoever says, 'You fool!' is in danger of hell's fire.

"If, therefore, you are presenting your offering at your place of worship and remember that your brother has a grudge against you, leave your offering there and first go to make peace; then come back and present your offering.

"Settle matters quickly with your accuser at law while you are with him on the way so he will not hand you over to the judge, who will turn you over to the guard, who will put you in prison. I tell you the truth, you will not be released until you have paid the last penny."

Sexual Sin

MATTHEW 5:27–32

Jesus continued, saying, "You have heard it said, 'You shall not commit adultery.' However, I say to you that if you look at a woman lustfully you have already committed adultery in your heart. If your right eye causes you to sin, pluck it out and throw it away—it is better to choose to live with one eye than for your entire body to be cast into hell. Likewise, if your right hand causes you to sin, cut it off and throw it away—it is better to choose to lose one part of your body than for your entire body to be cast into hell.

"It has also been said, 'If you divorce your wife you must give her a certificate of divorce.' However, if you divorce your wife, except for sexual unfaithfulness, you cause her to commit adultery, and anyone who marries her commits adultery."

False Vows

MATTHEW 5:33–37

Jesus continued, saying, "Again, you have heard it said to the people of old, 'Do not make false vows, but perform the vows you make to the Lord.' However, I tell you not to swear at all, either by heaven—it is the throne of God—or by the earth—it is God's footstool—or by Jerusalem—it is the city of the Great King. Also, do not swear by your head—you cannot make a single hair white or black. Just say yes or no—anything else comes from the evil one."

Love Enemies

MATTHEW 5:38–48; 7:12
LUKE 6:27–36

Jesus continued, saying, "Still again, you have heard it said, 'An eye for an eye and a tooth for a tooth.' Nevertheless, I say to you, do not resist the evil person who injures you—if he hits you on the right cheek, also turn to him the other one to hit. If someone wants to sue you in court and take your shirt, also give him your coat. In spite of this, I tell you to love your enemies, treat well those who hate you, bless those who curse you, and pray for those who mistreat you. Give to him who asks you, and do not refuse when someone wants to borrow from you. If anyone takes what belongs to you, do not demand it back. Treat people the way you want them to treat you.

"You have heard it said, 'Love your neighbor and hate your enemy.' On the other hand, I am telling you to love your enemies and pray for those who persecute you to show you are children of your Father in heaven. God causes the sun to rise on both the wicked and the good; He also causes it to rain on the righteous and the unrighteous.

"If you love those who love you, what credit is that to you and what reward will you get? Even the tax collectors—sinners—do the same thing; they love those who love them. If you are kind to those who are kind to you, what credit is that to you? Even sinners do the same thing. If you lend to those from whom you expect to be repaid, is that to your credit? Even sinners lend to sinners, expecting to be repaid. If you only greet your brothers—Gentiles do that—are you doing anything special?

"Consequently, you are to be perfect as your Father in heaven is perfect. Love your enemies, be kind to them, and lend to them without expecting payment. Then you will receive a great reward and will be sons of the Most High—He is kind to ungrateful and wicked men. Be merciful just as your Father is merciful. For that reason, do to others as you would like them to do to you, because this sums up the law and the prophets."

Proper Giving

MATTHEW 6:1–4

Jesus continued, saying, "Beware of practicing good works publicly in order to be noticed by others. If you do, your Father in heaven will not reward you. Therefore, when you give to the poor, do not proclaim it with fanfare as the hypocrites do in the synagogues and streets so they can be honored by men. I tell you the truth, that will be their only reward and recognition. Conversely, to please God, when you provide charity, do not let your left hand know what your right hand is doing—He sees what you do in secret and will reward you."

Correct Praying

MATTHEW 6:5–18
LUKE 11:1–4

Jesus continued, saying, "When you come to God in prayer, do not be like the hypocrites—they make a production of it in the synagogues and street corners to be noticed by men. I tell you the truth, they have their reward. When you pray, find a quiet, secluded place; pray to your unseen Father, Who sees what is done in secret—He will reward you. When you pray, do not use numerous and repetitious words like the Gentiles—they think they will be heard because of their many words. Do not be like them, because your Father knows better than you what you need even before you ask Him."

One day Jesus was praying in a certain place. When He finished, one of His disciples asked, "Lord, teach us to pray just as John taught his disciples."

So He said, "When you pray, say,

Our Father in heaven,
hallowed be Your name.
Your will be done
    on earth as it is in heaven.
Give us each day our daily bread.
Forgive us our debts of sin,
    as we forgive those who sin against us.
Lead us not into temptation,
    but deliver us from the evil one.
Yours is the kingdom, power, and glory forever.
Amen.

If you forgive others when they sin against you, your Father in heaven will also forgive you. However, if you do not forgive others for their sins, your Father will not forgive your sins.

"When you practice fasting, do not make a production out of it and look gloomy like the hypocrites—they neglect their appearance to make their fasting apparent to others. I tell you the truth, they have received their full reward. However, when you fast, look your best—wash your hair and face so it is not obvious to others that you are fasting except to your unseen Father, Who sees what is done in secret and will reward you."

No Worries

MATTHEW 6:19–34
LUKE 12:22–34

Jesus continued, saying, "Do not be fearful, little flock, because your Father has gladly chosen to give you the kingdom. Sell your possessions and donate it to charity. Do not heap up treasure down here on earth, but store up an inexhaustible treasure for yourselves in heaven that will not wear out, where moth and rust do not destroy and where thieves cannot break in and steal it. Your heart will be where you keep your treasure.

"The eye is the light of the body. If your eyes are wide open, your body fills up with light. However, if your eyes are bad, darkness will fill your body. Therefore, if the light in you is darkness, the darkness is indeed great.

"You cannot serve two masters at once. If you love one master you will end up hating the other. Devotion to one results in contempt for the other. You cannot serve both God and money."

Jesus continued this subject with His disciples, saying, "Therefore, I tell you not to worry about your life—what you will eat—or about your body—what you will wear—because there are more important things in life than food and clothes. Observe and consider the birds of the air; they neither sow nor reap nor store away in barns, and yet your Father in heaven feeds them.

"None of your worrying can add a single hour to your life. Since you are not able to do such a small thing, why do you worry about the rest?

"Why do you worry about clothes? Consider the lilies of the field; they grow and do not toil or spin. Yet I tell you that even Solomon in his entire splendor was not dressed like these flowers. Since that is how God clothes the grass of the field, which lives today and is thrown into the furnace tomorrow, will He not more surely clothe you who are of little faith? Therefore, do not be anxious about what you will eat, drink, or wear.

"Gentiles seek after these things, and your Father in heaven knows that you need them all. First seek His kingdom and righteousness; then all these things will also be given to you. Therefore, do not worry about tomorrow—it will take care of itself. Each day has sufficient trouble of its own."

Treating Others

MATTHEW 7:1–11
LUKE 6:37–42; 11:5–13

Jesus continued, saying, "Do not judge, criticize, and condemn others or you will be treated the same way—just as you do these things it will be done to you and in accordance with the measure used by you. Forgive and you will receive forgiveness. Give and it will be given back to you with bonus and blessing."

He further told them a parable, saying, "Can a blind man guide a blind man? Would not they both stumble and end up in the ditch? A pupil is not superior to his teacher, but everyone, when completely trained, will be like his teacher—so be careful who you follow as your teacher."

Jesus continued, saying, "It is easy to see a speck of sawdust in your brother's eye and be oblivious to the log in your own eye. Do you have the nerve to say, 'Let me wash the speck of sawdust from your eye for you,' when your own eye has a log in it? You hypocrite, first take the log out of your own eye so you can clearly see to remove the speck of sawdust from your brother's eye.

"Do not give holy and sacred things to dogs, and do not throw your pearls to pigs lest they step on them with their feet; then they will turn and tear you to pieces."

Then He said to them, "Imagine what would happen if you went to a friend at midnight and said, 'Friend, lend me three loaves of bread because an old friend traveling through just showed up and I do not have a thing to set before him.' Then the one inside answers, 'Do not bother me. The door is already locked and my children are with me in bed; I cannot get up to give you anything.' I tell you that even if he will not get up and give him anything because he is a friend, yet, because of his persistence, he will get up and give him as much as he needs.

"Here is what I am saying: Ask persistently and it will be given to you; seek persistently and you will find; knock persistently and the door will be opened for you.

"Who among you, if his son asks for bread will give him a stone? Or if he asks for a fish will give him a snake? Or if he asks for an egg will give him a scorpion? If you, then, even though you are evil, know how to give good gifts to your children, how much more will your Father in heaven give good gifts to those who ask Him—He will give the Holy Spirit to those who ask Him!"

Narrow Gate

MATTHEW 7:13–29
LUKE 6:43–49

Jesus continued, saying, "Enter through the narrow gate. Wide is the gate and broad is the road that leads to destruction—many enter through this easy way.

"Be wary of prophets—preachers—who come to you dressed like sheep but inside are ravenous wolves. You will recognize them by their fruits. Are grapes picked from thorn bushes and figs from thistles? Likewise, good trees bear good fruit, but decaying trees bear worthless fruit. A good tree cannot bear worthless fruit, and a decaying tree cannot bear good fruit. All trees that do not bear good fruit are cut down and cast into the fire. As a result, you will know them by their fruit.

"Not everyone who says to Me, 'Lord, Lord,' will enter the kingdom of heaven; only he who does the will of My Father Who is in heaven will enter the kingdom. Many will say to Me on that day, 'Lord, Lord, did we not prophesy—preach—in Your name and in Your name cast out demons and perform many miracles?' Then I will declare to them publicly, 'I never knew you. Depart from Me, you who acted wickedly.'

"You do not get bad fruit off a healthy tree or good fruit off a diseased tree. The health of the fruit provides recognition of the tree—figs are not gathered from thorn bushes or grapes from briers. The upright man, out of the good treasure in his heart, produces what is good, and the evil man, out of the evil stored in his heart, produces evil things—his mouth speaks from what fills his heart.

"Why do you call me 'Lord, Lord,' and not practice what I say? Everyone who comes to Me listens to My words and puts them into practice; I will show you what he is like. He may be compared to a wise man who built his house upon the rock—he dug deep and laid the foundation on the rock. The rain came down, the floods came, and the wind blew—the torrent struck the house—but the house did not shake because it was well built. Anyone who hears My words and does not put them into practice is like one who built a house on the ground without a foundation; when the torrent hit the house it immediately collapsed—it was completely destroyed."

When Jesus concluded His address, the crowds were amazed at His teaching because He taught as One with authority and not as their religion experts.

Three Healings

MATTHEW 8:5–13
LUKE 7:1–17
JOHN 4:46–54

When Jesus finished all that He had to say to the people, He went to Capernaum. A Roman centurion there had a servant, whom he highly regarded, who was sick and at the point of death. When the centurion heard about Jesus, he sent some Jewish elders to ask Him to come and heal his servant; they came to Jesus and urged Him to help, saying, "His servant lies at home paralyzed and in terrible pain. The centurion is worthy to have You do this because he loves our nation—he built us our synagogue."

Jesus said, "I will come and heal him."

Then He went with them. When He was not far from the house, the centurion sent friends to tell Him, "Lord, do not trouble Yourself, because I am not worthy to have You come under my roof. I did not come to You myself because I do not consider myself worthy. However, if You just speak, it will heal my servant. I know because I am a man under authority who takes orders and I also give orders to soldiers under me. I tell one soldier, 'Go,' and he goes; to another, 'Come,' and he comes; to my slave, 'Do this,' and he does it."

When Jesus heard this, He was amazed by the centurion and, turning to the crowd that was following Him, said, "I tell you the truth, I have not found so much faith in anyone, even in Israel. I tell you that many will come from east and west to sit at the table with Abraham, Isaac, and Jacob in the kingdom of heaven, but those who grew up in the faith and had no faith will be cast into outer darkness where there will be weeping and gnashing of teeth."

Then Jesus said to the men sent by the centurion, "Go, it will be done as believed by him." At that moment his servant became well. The men returned to the house and found the servant well.

Not long after that, Jesus went to the town Nain. His disciples and a large crowd went with Him. As they approached the town gate, a dead man—a woman's only son—was being carried out for burial. The mother was a widow. A sizeable crowd was with her. When Jesus saw her, He had compassion for her and said, "Do not cry." Then He went over and touched the coffin; those carrying it came to a stop. He said, "Young man, I tell you, get up!" The dead son sat up and began talking. Jesus gave him back to his mother.

Reverent fear gripped them all and they began praising God, saying, "A great Prophet has appeared among us," and, "God has come to visit and help His people." The news of Jesus spread throughout Judea and all the surrounding country.

Again He came to Cana of Galilee, the place where He made the water into wine. In Capernaum there was a certain royal official whose son was sick. When the official heard that Jesus had come from Judea to Galilee, he went and asked that He come down and heal his son, who was close to death.

Jesus told him, "Unless you people see signs and miracles, you refuse to believe."

The royal official pleaded with Him, saying, "Sir, come at once before my child dies."

Jesus replied, "Go home. Your son lives."

The man believed Jesus and headed home. Even as he was on his way back home, his servants met him and announced, "Your son lives!"

He asked them what time he began to get better. They said, "The fever broke yesterday afternoon at the seventh hour" (one o'clock in the afternoon). The father realized that was the exact moment Jesus had said, "Your son lives." As a result, he believed, along with his entire household.

This was now the second miracle Jesus performed after having come from Judea into Galilee.

Great John

MATTHEW 11:2–19
LUKE 7:18–35

When John, who was in prison, heard from his disciples what Jesus was doing, he sent two of them to the Lord to ask this question: "Are You the One we have been expecting or are we to wait on someone else?"

The men came before Jesus and said, "John the Baptist sent us to ask You, 'Are You the One we have been expecting or are we to wait on someone else?'"

At the same time, Jesus healed many from diseases, afflictions, and demons. He also gave sight to many who were blind. Jesus replied to the messengers, saying, "Go back and tell John what you have heard and seen: The blind see; the lame walk; the lepers are cured; the deaf hear; the dead are raised up; the poor are preached the good news. Blessed is the man who is not offended by Me."

As John's messengers departed, Jesus said more about John to the crowd, saying, "What did you go out into the desert to see? A reed swayed by the wind? What did you go out to see? A man dressed in soft clothes? Behold, those who are dressed in fine apparel and live in luxury are in the palaces of kings. What, then, did you go out to see? Did you go out to see a prophet? I tell you he is superior to a prophet. He is the one of whom it is written: 'I am sending my messenger' (prophet) 'ahead of You and he will prepare Your way before You.'

"I tell you the truth, of those born of women, there has not been raised anyone greater than John the Baptist. However, the most inferior in the kingdom of God is greater than he. All the people who heard Him, even the tax collectors, admitted God's justice because they had been baptized with the baptism of John. Still, the Pharisees and religion experts rejected God's purpose concerning them by refusing the baptism of John. From the time of John the Baptist until now, the kingdom of heaven has endured violence and violent men take it by force. For all the prophets and the law prophesied until John. If you care to accept it, John is Elijah who was to come. He who has ears, let him listen.

"So to what can I compare this generation? What are they like? They are like little children sitting in the marketplace calling to each other, saying, 'You did not dance when we played the flute for you, and you did not cry in mourning when we sang dirges for you.' John the Baptist came neither eating bread nor drinking wine and you say, 'He has a demon.' The son of Man came eating and drinking with others; then you say, 'He is a glutton and drunkard, along with being a friend of tax collectors and sinners.' However, wisdom is vindicated by her children—her actions."

Forgiving Sins

LUKE 7:36–50

One of the Pharisees invited Jesus over for dinner. He went to the Pharisee's house and reclined at the table. When a woman of the town, who lived a particularly sinful life, learned that Jesus was a guest in the house of the Pharisee, she brought perfume in an alabaster vial. As she stood behind Him at His feet, weeping, she began to wet His feet with her tears. She wiped His feet with her hair, kissed them, and anointed them with the perfume.

When the Pharisee who had invited Him saw this, he said to himself, "If this Man was the Prophet, He would surely know who and what sort of woman is touching Him."

Jesus replied and said to him, "Simon, I have something to tell you."

Simon responded, "Tell me, Teacher."

Jesus said, "Two men were in debt to a moneylender. One owed five hundred denarii" (wages for five hundred days) "and the other fifty. Neither of them was able to repay, and the moneylender canceled both debts. Which of the two would love him more?"

Simon replied, "I suppose the one who had the bigger debt canceled."

"You have decided correctly," Jesus said.

Then, turning to the woman but speaking to Simon, He said, "Do you see this woman? I came into your house. You did not provide Me with water for My feet, but she wet my feet with her tears and dried them with her hair. You did not greet Me with a kiss, but this woman, from the time I entered your house, has not ceased kissing My feet. You did not anoint My head with oil, but she has anointed My feet with expensive perfume. As a result, I tell you she has been forgiven of her many sins because she has loved much. On the other hand, he who is forgiven little loves little."

Then Jesus said to her, "Your sins are forgiven."

The other dinner guests began talking among themselves, saying, "Who is this Man Who even forgives sins? Who does He think He is, forgiving sins?"

Jesus said to the woman, "Your faith has saved you. Go in peace."

Divided House

MATTHEW 12:22–37
MARK 3:20–30
LUKE 11:14–23

Jesus came home and a crowd gathered—He and His disciples could not even eat. When His family heard what was going on, they went to take Him by force—they said, "He is out of His mind."

There was brought to Jesus a demon-possessed man—the demon kept the man blind and mute. Jesus cast out the demon from the man that kept him mute; He healed him—gave him his speech and sight.

With the demon gone, the man started talking; the crowd was amazed and said, "Can He be the Son of David?" Some from the crowd, the Pharisees and religion experts from Jerusalem, when they heard the report, said, "This Man drives out demons because He is helped by Beelzebub, the prince of demons—He is possessed by Beelzebub." Others tested Him by demanding a miracle from heaven.

Jesus, knowing what they were thinking, spoke to them in parables, saying, "How can Satan cast out Satan? Any kingdom that is divided against itself will be ruined and is unable to stand—a house divided against itself will fall. If Satan opposes himself—is divided against himself—he cannot stand and is finished in effectiveness. You accuse Me of casting out demons by Beelzebub. If I cast out demons with the help of Beelzebub, by whom do the people who follow you cast them out? For this reason they will be your judges. On the other hand, if I cast out demons by the finger and Spirit of God, then God's kingdom has come to you.

"How can anyone go into a strong man's house and take his property without first tying up the strong man? When a strong man, who is fully armed, guards his own house, his possessions are safe. Conversely, when he is attacked by someone stronger, he is overpowered and the armor in which he trusted is taken away and divided up as plunder.

"He who is not with Me, is against Me, and he who does not gather for My side scatters. I tell you the truth, every sin and blasphemy can be forgiven of men. However, whoever blasphemes against the Holy Spirit will never be forgiven. Whoever speaks against the Son of Man can be forgiven, but anyone who speaks against and blasphemes the Holy Spirit will not be forgiven either in this age or the age to come." He said this because they persisted in saying, "He has a demon."

Jesus continued, saying, "If you grow a healthy tree, its fruit will be good, and if you grow a diseased tree, its fruit will be bad—the tree is known by its fruit. You offspring of snakes! How can what you say be worth anything when you are evil? Your mouth speaks what overflows from your heart. A good man produces good things from the good stored in him, and the evil man produces evil things from the evil stored in him. However, I tell you that men, on judgment day, will have to give an account for every little careless word they have spoken during their lives. By your words you will be justified, and by your words you will be condemned at judgment."

Jonah Sign

MATTHEW 12:38–45
LUKE 11:24–36

Then some of the religion experts and Pharisees said to Him, "Teacher, we want to see a miracle proving Your claim."

As the crowd increased, Jesus replied to them, "This is a wicked and adulterous generation asking for a sign, but no sign shall be given it except the sign of the prophet Jonah. The only proof you are going to receive is the proof he gave to the Ninevites. Just as Jonah was in the belly of a huge sea creature three days and nights, so will the Son of Man be three days and nights in the heart of the earth. Just as Jonah was a sign to the Ninevites, likewise will the Son of Man be to this generation. On judgment day, the Ninevites will stand up and give evidence that will condemn this generation, because they repented when Jonah preached to them. Behold, Someone greater than Jonah is here. At the judgment, the Queen of the South will come forward condemning this generation, because she came from the ends of the earth to listen to Solomon's wisdom. Now One greater than Solomon is here.

"No one lights a lamp and then puts it in a cellar or a place where it will be hidden. Instead, it is put on a stand so those entering the room have light to see. Your eye is the lamp of your body. When your eye is clear, your body fills up with light, but when your eye is not clear, your body is filled with darkness. Therefore, if your entire body is full of light with no part of it dark, it will be completely lit as when a lamp gives you light.

"When a demon comes out of a man, it roams through arid places in search of rest but does not find it. Then it says, 'I will return to the person I left.' Upon arrival, it finds the person swept clean and orderly but vacant. It then runs out and rounds up seven other demons more wicked than it and they live there. That person ends up in worse condition than in the first place. That is how it will be with this wicked generation."

While He was saying these things, a woman in the crowd raised her voice and said, "Blessed is the woman who gave You birth and breasts that nursed You."

Jesus replied, "Even more blessed are those who hear the word of God and obey it by practicing it."

Jesus' Family

MATTHEW 12:46–50
MARK 3:31–35
LUKE 8:19–21

While Jesus was still talking to the crowd, His mother, brothers, and sisters came to see and speak to Him but could not get through to Him because of the crowd—He was surrounded by the crowd. They were standing outside and sent someone to relay a message that they wanted a word with Him. Someone in the crowd said to Jesus, "Your mother, brothers, and sisters are outside looking for You and want to speak with You."

Jesus asked, "Who are My mother, brothers, and sisters?" Looking at those seated in a circle around Him, He pointed to His disciples and said, "These are My mother, brothers, and sisters—the ones who hear and put into practice the will of God."

Seed Parable

MATTHEW 13:1–9
MARK 4:1–9
LUKE 8:1–8

Soon afterward, Jesus traveled from one town and village to another, proclaiming and preaching the good news of the kingdom. The Twelve were with Him along with some women of God who had been cured of demons and diseases: Mary, the one called Magdalene, from whom seven demons had come out; Joanna, wife of Chuza, Herod's household manager; Susanna—along with many others who contributed to their support out of their private means.

That same day Jesus left the house and sat by the lake. The large crowd that gathered around Him forced Him to get into a boat and sit in it out on the lake, while the people gathered and stood along the shore at the water's edge. While a large crowd was gathering to Him from town after town, He taught them many things using parables. He said, "A farmer went out and planted his seed. As he scattered the seed, some of it fell on the path; it was trampled down and the birds came and ate it. Some fell in rocky places; it sprouted quickly but did not put down roots, so when the sun came up the plants were scorched and they withered due to lack of moisture in the shallow soil. Some fell among thorns; as it came up and grew among the thorns, it was choked by the thorns and they did not bear a crop. Still other seed fell on good soil and produced a crop, multiplying thirty, sixty, or even a hundred times more than was sown originally."

After telling this parable, Jesus said, "He who has ears, let him listen and understand."

Why Parables

MATTHEW 13:10–17
MARK 4:10–12
LUKE 8:9–10

When they were alone, those who were around Jesus with the twelve apostles asked Him about the parables and what this parable meant, saying, "Why do You speak to the people in parables?"

Jesus replied, "You have been granted to know the secret of the kingdom of heaven and its mysteries but not to those on the outside of our circle. For them, everything is said in parables so that

Though they see, they do not perceive;
though they hear, they do not understand.
Otherwise, they might turn from their willful rejection of the truth
    and be forgiven.

In them the prophecy of Isaiah is fulfilled:

You shall indeed hear but not understand;
you shall indeed see but not perceive.
This nation's heart has become calloused;
they barely hear with their ears
and they have closed their eyes.
Otherwise, they might perceive with their eyes,
comprehend with their ears,
understand with their heart,
and turn from their rejection of truth,
which would result in My healing them.

On the other hand, you are blessed because you have eyes that see and ears that hear. I tell you the truth, many prophets and righteous men desired to see what you are seeing but did not see it, and to hear what you are hearing but did not hear it."

Parable Meaning

MATTHEW 13:18–23
MARK 4:13–20
LUKE 8:11–15

Jesus continued, saying, "Do you not understand this parable? How will you understand any parable? This is the meaning of the parable—this is what the parable of the sower means. The seed is the word of God. The seeds on the path are those who hear the word of God. When anyone hears news of the kingdom and does not understand, it just remains on the surface. No sooner do they hear the Word than the Evil One" (Satan) "comes along and snatches away what has been planted in them; he takes away what has been planted in their hearts so that they do not believe and are not saved from their sins.

"The seed that is planted and lands in rocky places is the person who hears the Word and instantly responds with joy, but the enthusiasm does not last long because they have no root. There is little or shallow soil of character; therefore, when emotions wear off and some difficulty—time of trial and temptation—arrives, they last only a short time and quickly fall away.

"The seed planted in the thorns represents the person who hears the kingdom news, but the worries of this life and the deceitfulness of wealth choke the word and make it unfruitful—stress strangles what was heard, the seed is crowded out, and it does not mature.

"However, the seed planted on good soil represents those with an honest and good heart who hear the Word. They take it in, understand it, accept it, and embrace it—they produce a crop that yields a hundred, sixty, or thirty times what was planted originally."

Unhidden Lamp

MARK 4:21–25
LUKE 8:16–18

Jesus continued, saying, "Does anyone bring a lamp to put it under a bowl or under a bed? Instead, you put it on a stand in order that those who come in may see the light. There is nothing hidden that is not meant to be revealed and nothing concealed that is not meant to come into the light. If a man has ears, let him comprehend. Consequently, be careful how you listen. The standard of measure you use will be the standard used to measure you—even more shall be given you besides. To him who has will be given more, and whoever does not have, even what he has will be taken away."

Unending Parables

MATTHEW 13:24–35
MARK 4:26–34
LUKE 13:18–21

Jesus told them another parable, saying, "The kingdom of heaven is like a man who planted good seed in his field. However, while everyone was sleeping, his enemy came and planted weeds among the wheat and went away. When the wheat grew and produced heads of grain, the weeds appeared too.

"The servants of the owner came to him and said, 'Sir, did you not plant good seed in your field? Why, then, are there weeds in it?'

"He answered, 'An enemy did this.'

"The servants asked, 'Do you want us to pull the weeds out?'

"He said, 'No, because you may pull out the wheat when you pull out the weeds. Let them grow together until harvest time. Then I will tell the harvesters to pull up the weeds and tie them in bundles to be burned, then gather the wheat and put it in my barn.'"

Then Jesus said, "The kingdom of heaven is like seed scattered on the ground by a man who continues sleeping at night and arising at day while the seed sprouts up and grows—he does not know how it happens. The soil does it all without his help—first the blade, then the head, and then the ripened grain. As soon as the grain is ripe, he uses the sickle because the harvest is ready."

He told them another parable, saying, "What is the kingdom of God like and to what shall I compare it? What parable shall we use to explain it? It is like a mustard seed, which is the smallest seed planted in the soil by man in his garden. However, when it grows, it becomes the largest of garden plants—it becomes a tree with branches big enough for birds of the air to make a nest in its shade."

Again, He told them another parable, saying, "To what shall I compare the kingdom of God? It is like yeast that a woman took and mixed into three measures of flour until the yeast was throughout the dough."

All these things Jesus spoke to the crowd in parables—He said nothing to them without a parable. This fulfilled what was spoken by the prophet:

I will open My mouth and tell parables,
I will utter things hidden since the creation of the world.

With many parables like these He spoke to them. When He was alone with His disciples, He explained everything to them.

End Times

MATTHEW 13:36–52

Then Jesus left the crowd and went into the house. His disciples came to Him and said, "Explain to us that parable of the weeds in the field."

He answered, saying, "The One Who planted the good seed is the Son of Man. The field is the world, the good seeds are the children of the kingdom, and the weeds are the children of the evil one—the enemy who plants them is the devil. The harvest is the end of the age, and the harvesters are angels.

"Just as the weeds are pulled up and burned, so it will be at the end of the age. The Son of Man will send His angels; they will gather out of His kingdom all stumbling blocks that cause sin and those who do evil. They will cast them into the fiery furnace—a place where there will be weeping and grinding of teeth. At the same time the righteous will shine like the sun in the kingdom of their Father. Let him who has ears understand.

"The kingdom of heaven is like a treasure hidden in a field. When a man found it he hid it again. Then, in his joy, he proceeds to sell everything he owns to raise money and buy that field.

"Again, the kingdom of heaven is like a merchant seeking precious pearls. When he found a valuable one, he went and sold all he had and bought it.

"Again, the kingdom of heaven is like a net cast into the sea and catching all kinds of fish. When it is full, the fishermen haul it onto shore where they sit down and gather the good fish into containers, but the bad ones they throw away. That is how it will be at the end of the age—angels will come and separate the wicked from among the righteous and throw them into the fiery furnace, where there will be weeping and grinding of teeth."

Jesus asked, "Are you understanding all this?"

They answered, "Yes."

He said to them, "Hence, every religion expert who has been trained for the kingdom of heaven and becomes a disciple is like the head of the household who brings out of his storehouse treasure things that are new as well as old."

Have Faith

MATTHEW 8:23–27
MARK 4:35–41
LUKE 8:22–25

That day, in the evening, He said to His disciples, "Let us go over to the other side of the lake." When He got into the boat, His disciples followed Him. Leaving the crowd, they took Him just as He was and set out in the boat. Other boats came along with Him. As they were sailing, He fell asleep. A fierce storm came up on the lake. Waves swept over the boat so much that it was filling up—they were in great danger. Jesus was in the stern, with His head on a cushion, sleeping. The disciples woke Him, saying, "Lord, save us! Teacher, do you not care that we are going down? Master, Master, we are perishing!"

Awake now, Jesus replied, "Why are you so afraid?" Then He stood up and, rebuking the wind and raging waves, said, "Be still! Be silent!" The wind ceased and the water became calm. Jesus continued to reprimand His disciples, saying, "Why are you so afraid? How is it you lack faith in Me?"

Terrified and amazed, they asked each other, "Who is He? What kind of Man is He? He commands the wind and the sea—they obey Him."

Demon Legion

MATTHEW 8:28–34
MARK 5:1–20
LUKE 8:26–39

They sailed across the sea and, when they arrived at the other side, they came to the country of Gadarenes (Gerasenes), which is opposite Galilee. As soon as Jesus got out of the boat, when He stepped ashore, two men from the town, who were controlled by demons, came from the tombs—they lived in the tombs—and met Him. They had not worn clothes for a long time or lived in a house. The demons had seized them many times. No one could subdue them any longer, even with a chain. They had often been bound with shackles on the feet and chains on the hands, plus being kept under guard, but they tore the chains apart and broke the shackles on their feet. They had been driven by the demons into the desert. No one was strong enough to subdue them. Night and day they roamed among the tombs and on the mountains, screaming out and slashing themselves with sharp stones. The men were so violent that no one was able to pass that way.

When they saw Jesus from a distance, they ran to Him, screamed, and fell down before Him. One of the madmen said loudly, "What do You want with us, Jesus, Son of the Most High God? Have You come to torment me before the appointed time? I beg You by God not to torment me!" The man said this because Jesus had just started to command the demon, saying, "Demon, come out of the man!"

Jesus asked him, "What is your name?"

He replied, "Legion. My name is Legion because we are many." He said this because many demons had gone into him. The demons begged Jesus repeatedly not to order them to the bottomless pit. They repeatedly begged Jesus not to command them to leave that region.

At some distance from there a large herd of pigs was feeding on a nearby hillside. The demons begged Jesus, saying, "If You drive us out of these men, send us to the pigs."

Jesus gave them permission, saying, "Go!" The demons came out of the men and into the pigs. The entire herd of about two thousand rushed down the steep bank into the lake and drowned—they died in the water.

When those tending the pigs saw what happened, they ran off and told everyone back in the town and the countryside their story—what had happened to the men possessed with demons and the pigs. Everyone wanted to see what had happened—people went out to see for themselves. The entire town went out to meet Jesus and saw the man who had been possessed by a legion of demons. They found the man sitting at the feet of Jesus, clothed and in his right mind—they were afraid.

Those who had seen it told the people what had happened to the demon-possessed man and the pigs—how he had been restored to health. Later, a great many people from the country of the Gerasene pleaded with Him to leave their region because they were overcome with great fear. Jesus got into the boat and left.

As Jesus was getting into the boat, the man who had been possessed by demons begged to go with Him, but He would not let him. Jesus sent him back, saying, "Go home to your own people and tell them how much the Lord has done for you and how He had mercy on you." So the man departed and began to proclaim in Decapolis what Jesus had done for him. All the people were astonished when they heard the story.

Girl Raised

MATTHEW 9:18–26
MARK 5:21–43
LUKE 8:40–56

When Jesus finished saying this, after He crossed over by boat to the other side, a large crowd gathered around Him at the seashore and welcomed His return—they were all waiting for Him. A local official, one of the synagogue leaders, a man named Jairus, came and, when he saw Jesus, bowed, fell at His feet, and knelt before Him, begging Him to come to his house because his only daughter, who was twelve years old, was dying. He said, "My dear daughter is dying. If You come and lay Your hands on her, she will be healed and live." Jesus got up and went with him, making His way through the pushing crowd that pressed Him; His disciples accompanied Him.

Just then there was in the crowd that day a woman who had been hemorrhaging for twelve years. She had endured a great amount of suffering at the hands of many physicians and spent all her money on them, but none of them could heal her—she got worse instead of better. She had heard about Jesus, came up behind Him, and touched the tassel of His robe. She kept thinking to herself, "If I can just touch His robe,

I will be restored to health." Immediately, her hemorrhaging stopped and she felt her body was healed of the ailment. At the same moment, Jesus realized that power had proceeded from Him. He turned around in the crowd and asked, "Who touched Me? Who touched My robe?" His disciples said, "With this crowd pushing You from all sides, You ask 'Who touched Me?'" When everyone denied touching Him, Peter said, "Master, the people are crowding and pressing against You." Jesus insisted, "Someone touched Me. I felt power go out from Me." Jesus kept looking around to see who had done it. The woman, realizing that she could not escape notice and also knowing what had been done for her, came frightened and trembling to Jesus, fell down before His feet, and told Him the whole truth—why she touched Him and how she was healed at the same moment. Then He said to her, "Courage, daughter. Your faith has healed you. Go in peace and be continually free from your disease."

While He was still speaking, some people came from the synagogue leader's house and told him, "Your daughter has died and there is no need to bother the Teacher anymore." Jesus overheard but ignored what they were talking about and said to the leader, "Do not be alarmed and fearful; only believe." When Jesus arrived at the leader's house and saw the flute players and the noisy crowd—they were crying and mourning for her—He permitted no one to go in with Him except Peter, James, John, and the child's father and mother. Jesus said, "Why do you make a commotion and cry? Stop it and go away. The girl is not dead but asleep." They laughed at Him with scorn because they knew she was dead. After He put them all outside, He took the child's father and mother, along with His companions, and entered the room where the girl was lying. He gripped the girl's hand firmly and said to her, "*Talitha koum*," which means, "Little girl, get up." Her spirit returned and she immediately stood up and started walking around, for she was twelve years old. Jesus commanded them not to tell anyone about this. Then He directed them to give her something to eat. The news of this event spread through the entire region.

Blind Men

MATTHEW 9:27–34

As Jesus left that house, two blind men followed Him, shouting, "Have pity on us, Son of David!"

When Jesus arrived at the house and went in, the blind men went in to Him. Jesus asked them, "Do you believe I can do this?"

They replied, "Yes, Lord!"

Then He touched their eyes and said, "According to your faith, let it be done to you." Their sight was restored to them. Jesus sternly warned them, saying, "Do not let anyone know about this!" However, they went out and spread the news about Him over the entire region.

As they were leaving, a man who had been struck speechless by a demon was brought to Jesus. As soon as Jesus drove the demon out, the man spoke, which caused the crowd to be stunned with bewilderment. They said, "Nothing like this has ever been seen in Israel." However, the Pharisees said, "He drives out demons by the prince of demons."

Prophet Honor

MATTHEW 13:53–58
MARK 6:1–6

When Jesus finished telling parables, He left there and went to His hometown; His disciples accompanied Him. On the Sabbath, He taught in their synagogue. They were amazed and said, "Where did He acquire these things? Where did this Man get this wisdom that has been given to Him? Miracles are even done by His hands! Is this not the carpenter and the Son of a carpenter? Is He not the Son of Mary and are not His brothers James, Joseph" (Joses), "Judas" (Judah), "and Simon? Do not His sisters live with us?" They took offense at Him—they stumbled and fell over what they knew about Him.

Jesus told them, "A prophet is taken for granted; he has little honor in his hometown and in his own house."

He could not do many miracles there because of their unbelief, except to lay hands on a few sick people and cure them. Jesus marveled at their unbelief. He left and made a teaching circuit of the other towns.

Always Working

JOHN 5:1–18

Later on, Jesus went up to Jerusalem for a Jewish feast. Near the Sheep Gate in Jerusalem there is a pool, which is called Bethesda, with five porches in which lay a multitude of sick, blind, crippled, and paralyzed people waiting for the bubbling of the water—an angel of the Lord went down at certain times into the pool and stirred up the water. Whoever first stepped into the stirred-up water was made well—was cured of any afflicting disease. One man had been an invalid there for thirty-eight years. When Jesus saw him lying there and knowing how long he had been there in that condition, He said, "Do you want to get well?"

The invalid said, "Sir, when the water is stirred, I do not have anybody to help me into the pool. By the time I get there, somebody else steps down ahead of me."

Jesus said to him, "Get up, take your sleeping mat and walk." Immediately the man was cured; he picked up his sleeping mat and began to walk around.

The day this happened was the Sabbath. The Jews kept saying to the cured man, "It is the Sabbath. The law forbids you to carry your sleeping mat."

He answered them, saying, "The Man Who cured me said, 'Take your sleeping mat and walk.'"

They asked him, "Who is the Man Who told you to take it and start walking?" However, the cured man did not know, because Jesus had slipped away into the crowd.

A little later, Jesus found him in the temple and said to him, "See, you have become well. Stop sinning or something worse might happen to you." The man went away and told the Jews that it was Jesus Who had cured him. That is why the Jews began to persecute Jesus—because He was doing these things. Nevertheless, Jesus answered them, saying, "My Father is always working and so am I." For this reason the Jews were more determined to kill Him. Not only was He breaking the Sabbath but He was calling God His own Father, putting Himself equal with God.

True Testimony

JOHN 5:19–47

Then Jesus answered them, saying, "I tell you the truth, the Son can do nothing by Himself but is only able to do what He sees the Father doing, because whatever the Father does the Son does in the same manner. The Father loves the Son and shows Him everything He is doing Himself. Greater things than these He will show Him so that you may marvel. Just as the Father raises the dead and gives them life, so the Son gives life to whomever He wishes. The Father does not judge anyone, because He has given all judgment to the Son in order that all men may honor the Son just as they give honor to the Father. Whoever does not honor the Son does not honor the Father who sent Him.

"I tell you the truth, anyone who hears My words and believes Him Who sent Me has eternal life—they will not be condemned and he has already passed out of death into life. I tell you the truth, the time is coming, and is now here, when the dead will hear the voice of the Son of God—those who hear it shall live. Just as the Father has life in Himself, He has given the Son life in Himself, and He has given Him the authority to judge because He is the Son of Man.

"Do not be surprised at this, because the time is coming when everyone in the graves will hear His voice and come out—those who have practiced doing good will be resurrected to life, and those who have practiced evil will be resurrected to damnation.

"I can do nothing by Myself; I judge only as I hear from God. My judgment is just because I do not seek My own will but the will of the

Father Who sent Me. If I alone testify about Myself, My testimony is not valid.

"You have sent an inquiry to John and he has testified to the truth. However, the witness I accept is not from man, but I say these things so that you may receive salvation. John was a lamp that kept burning and gave you light—you chose for a while to delight yourselves in his light.

"Nevertheless, I have a witness greater than John because the work the Father has appointed for Me to accomplish, which I am doing now, testifies that the Father has sent Me. The Father Who sent Me has testified Himself concerning Me. No one has heard His voice or seen His form. His Word does not live in you because you do not believe Him Whom He sent to you. You search and study the Scriptures because you think that by them you have eternal life. These very Scriptures testify about Me and still you refuse to come to Me so that you may have life.

"I do not crave or accept praise from men. I know you—you do not have the love of God in you. I came with the authority of My Father's name and you did not accept Me. However, if someone else comes in his own name, you will accept him. How is it possible for you to believe when you are content to accept praise from one another and you do not seek the praise that comes from the only God?

"However, do not think I am going to accuse you before the Father. Moses, in whom you have built your hopes, is your accuser. If you believed Moses, you would believe Me because he wrote about Me. Yet, if you do not believe what he wrote, how will you believe Me?"

Plentiful Harvest

MATTHEW 9:35–10:28
MARK 6:7–13
LUKE 9:1–6

Jesus made a circuit of all the towns and villages, teaching in their synagogues, preaching the good news of the kingdom and curing every kind of disease and sickness. When He saw the crowds, He felt compassion for them because they were helpless like sheep without a shepherd. Then He said to His disciples, "The harvest is plenty but the workers are few. For that reason, pray the Lord of the harvest to send out workers into the harvest."

Jesus summoned to Him His twelve disciples. He sent them out in pairs and gave them authority and power to drive out demons, to cure diseases and sickness, and to preach the kingdom of God. This is the list of the twelve apostles He sent:

Simon (who is called Peter),
Andrew (his brother),
James (Zebedee's son),
John (his brother),
Philip,
Bartholomew,
Thomas,
Matthew (the tax collector),
James (son of Alphaeus),
Thaddaeus,
Simon (the Canaanite), and
Judas Iscariot (the one who betrayed Him).

Jesus sent out these twelve with the following instructions:

"Do not go among the Gentiles and do not go to any Samaritan town. Go to the lost sheep of the house of Israel. As you go, preach, saying, 'The kingdom of heaven is at hand.' Cure the sick, raise the dead, cleanse the lepers, and cast out demons. You received freely; give freely. Do not take gold, silver, or copper money for your purse. Do not take a bag of provisions or food for your journey or extra undergarments, sandals, or staff, because the worker is deserving of his support.

"When you enter a town or village, inquire who there is worthy and stay at that person's house until you leave. When you go to the house, be courteous in your greeting. If they welcome you, the house is worthy—let your greeting of peace come upon it; nevertheless, if they do not welcome you or listen to your message, leave that house or town—shake the dust off your feet as a testimony against them. I tell you the truth, it will be more bearable for the land of Sodom and Gomorrah on the day of judgment than for that town. I am sending you out as sheep in the midst of wolves. For that reason, be as wise as snakes and as harmless as doves.

"Be on your guard against men whose nature is to act in opposition to God, because they will hand you over to the courts and flog you in their synagogues. You will be brought before governors and kings because of Me to give testimony to them and to the Gentiles. However, when they arrest you, do not worry about how or what you will speak, because the Spirit of your Father will give you, at that very moment, what you are to say to them.

"Brother will betray brother to death and the father his child. Children will rebel against their parents and will have them put to death. Everyone will hate you because of Me, but he who endures to the end will receive salvation. When you are persecuted in one town, flee to another town. I tell you the truth, you shall not finish going through the towns of Israel before the Son of Man comes.

"A student is neither above his teacher nor a servant above his master. It is sufficient for a student to be like his teacher and the servant like his master. If they call the Head of the house Beelzebub, they will call members of the household much more!

"Consequently, do not fear them, because nothing is concealed that will not be revealed or hidden that will not be made known. What I tell you in the dark, say in the light. What is whispered in your ear, proclaim on the housetops. Do not fear those who kill the body but not the soul. Fear the One Who can destroy both body and soul in hell."

They left and went from town to town preaching the Gospel and healing people everywhere. They preached that people should repent.

They drove out demons and anointed with oil many who were sick and cured them.

Man's Worth

MATTHEW 10:29—11:1

Jesus continued, saying, "Are not two sparrows sold for a penny? Yet, not one of them will fall to the ground outside the will of your Father. He pays even greater attention to you—He even numbers the hairs of your head. Therefore, do not be afraid. You are more valuable than many sparrows.

"Everyone who acknowledges and confesses Me before men, I will also acknowledge him before My Father in heaven. However, whoever decries and disowns Me before men, I will disown him before My Father in heaven.

"Do not think that I have come to bring peace to the earth. I have not come to bring peace but a sword. I have come to set a man against his father, a daughter against her mother, and a daughter-in-law against her mother-in-law—a man's enemies will be members of his own household.

"Anyone who loves father and mother more than Me is not worthy of Me; anyone who does not take up his cross and follow after Me is not worthy of Me. Whoever finds his life will lose it; whoever loses his life on My account will find it.

"Anyone who accepts what you do accepts Me. Anyone who accepts Me accepts Him Who sent Me. Anyone who accepts a prophet because he is a prophet will receive a prophet's reward; anyone who accepts a righteous man because he is a righteous man will receive a righteous man's reward. If anyone gives even a cup of cold water to one of these little ones in rank or influence because he is My disciple, I tell you the truth, he will definitely not lose his reward."

John's Death

MATTHEW 14:1–12
MARK 6:14–29
LUKE 3:19–20; 9:7–9

At that time, Herod, the governor, heard about the fame of Jesus because His name had become well known. When he heard what was being done by Jesus, he was perplexed and troubled by it. He said to his servants, "This is John the Baptist raised from the dead! That is why the power to perform miracles is at work in Him!"

There were people saying, "John has been raised from the dead."

Others said, "He is Elijah who has appeared to us."

Still others said, "He is a prophet from long ago risen back to life, or he is like one of those prophets."

However, Herod said, "I beheaded John. So, who is this that I keep hearing about? It has to be John raised from the dead!" Herod looked for a chance to see Him.

Herod was the one who had ordered the arrest of John—bound him and put him in prison—to appease Herodias, his brother Philip's wife, whom he had married, because John had been saying, "You are committing adultery." John had repeatedly reproved Herod for this and added it to all the other wicked things he had done in his life. Herod wanted to kill John because Herodias held a grudge against John and wanted him put to death. He was afraid to do so and protected him because the people regarded John as a prophet and because he was in awe of him, knowing he was a righteous and holy man. Herod was perplexed when he heard John but enjoyed listening to him.

Nonetheless, an opportune day arrived on Herod's birthday. He gave a banquet for his nobles, military commanders, and leading men of Galilee. Herodias' daughter entered the banquet hall and danced for them. She pleased Herod and the guests. She fascinated Herod so much that he promised her on oath anything she wanted from him. The king said to the girl, "Ask me for anything you want and I will give it to you."

He swore to her, "Whatever you ask of me I will give to you up to half of my kingdom." She went back to her mother and said, "What should I ask for from him?" Her mother said, "Ask for the head of John the Baptist." With this prompting from her mother, she excitedly rushed back to the king and said, "I want you to give me the head of John the Baptist on a platter and I want it right now." The king was sorry, but, because of his oaths and being unwilling to lose face with his guests, he immediately ordered John's head cut off and presented to the girl on a platter. The executioner went, cut off John's head, brought it back on a platter, and presented it to the girl; she brought it to her mother. When John's disciples heard about this, they came, took the body, and buried it in a tomb. Then they went and told Jesus.

Five Thousand

MATTHEW 14:13–21
MARK 6:30–44
LUKE 9:10–17
JOHN 6:1–15

After this, when Jesus heard this news, He withdrew from there by boat to a solitary place by Himself. The apostles had gathered together with Him and reported on all that they had done and taught. Jesus took them with Him and withdrew by themselves, near the town Bethsaida, to rest because there was a constant coming and going of people—they did not even have time to eat. Jesus said, "Come away by yourselves with Me to a quiet place for awhile." However, when the crowds heard about it—many saw and recognized them when they were leaving—they followed Him on foot from the towns. Jesus crossed to the other side of the Sea of Galilee (some call it Tiberias). The huge crowd followed Him because they had seen the miracles He performed on the sick. A lot of people got there ahead of them. When He landed on the other side, He went up on the side of a mountain and sat down with His disciples. The Passover, a feast of the Jews, was near. When Jesus saw the crowd,

He felt compassion for them because they were like sheep without a shepherd. He spoke to them about the kingdom of God—taught them many things—and He healed those who needed healing.

As the day declined, toward evening, His disciples—the Twelve—came to Him and said, "This is a desolate place and it is getting very late. Send the crowd away so they can go to the nearby towns and surrounding countryside to buy food and find lodging because this is a barren place."

However, Jesus replied, "They do not need to go away." When He looked out and saw the large crowd, Jesus said to Philip, "Where can we buy bread for these people to eat?" He said this to test him; He already knew what He intended to do for the people. Philip answered, "Two hundred denarii worth of bread would not be enough for each person to get a little piece!" Jesus replied, "You give them something to eat." They replied, "Shall we go and buy eight months' wages worth of bread to give them something to eat?" Jesus said, "How many loaves of bread do you have? Go and find out."

When they found out, one of the disciples (Andrew, brother of Simon Peter) said, "There is a boy here who has only five loaves of bread and two fish, but they will not go far among so many people; we will have to go and buy food for this crowd."

Jesus directed His disciples, saying, "Bring the food here to Me. Have the people sit down in groups of about fifty each." There was plenty of thick green grass in that place—they sat down in groups of fifty or a hundred. They looked like garden plots with the regularity of beds of herbs. He took the five loaves, lifted His face in prayer to heaven and gave thanks for it, broke it, and kept giving the bread to the disciples to hand out to the crowd. He did the same with the two fish when He gave thanks for them and divided them. Then the disciples gave the food to the people. They all ate as much as they wanted—they ate their fill. After the people had enough to eat, He said to His disciples, "So nothing is wasted, gather the leftovers." The disciples gathered them—they picked up twelve baskets of leftovers from the five barley loaves and two fish. About five thousand men ate, not including women and children.

When the people saw the miracle performed by Jesus, they said, "Undoubtedly, this is the Prophet Who is to come into the world!" Jesus, knowing they intended to forcefully make Him king, again withdrew to the mountainside by Himself.

Water Walking

MATTHEW 14:22–33
MARK 6:45–52
JOHN 6:16–21

Immediately (it was evening), Jesus insisted that the disciples get into the boat and go on ahead of Him to the other side, across from Bethsaida, while He dismissed the crowd. His disciples went down to the sea, got into the boat, and were going across the sea to Capernaum. After sending His disciples off, He dispersed the crowd and climbed the mountainside to be by Himself and pray. When it was evening, He was there alone.

Meanwhile, it was now dark and Jesus had not yet returned to them. By this time, the boat was far out to sea—it was in the middle of the sea—being battered by the waves and the strong wind. Jesus, alone on the land, saw His men struggling with the oars because the sea was against them and they were battered by the waves. During the fourth watch of the night—between three and six o'clock—when they had rowed three or four miles out, they saw Jesus walking on the water and approaching near the boat. It appeared He intended to go right by them. However, when they saw Him walking on the sea, they thought it was a ghost and cried out in terror, "It is a ghost!"

Jesus immediately spoke to them, saying, "Take courage, it is I. Do not be afraid."

Peter answered, "Lord, if it is You, command me to come to You on the water."

Jesus said, "Come."

Peter got out of the boat and walked on the water to Jesus. Nevertheless, when he saw and felt the strong wind, he became afraid and started to sink. He cried, "Lord, save me!"

Immediately, Jesus reached out His hand and grabbed him. Then He said, "You of little faith, why did you doubt?"

When the two of them climbed onboard the boat, the wind stopped blowing. Then the disciples in the boat, having watched the whole thing, were amazed beyond measure because they did not consider the miracle with the loaves—their hardened hearts did not allow them to understand. They worshiped Jesus, saying, "You are truly the Son of God!" Immediately, they reached the shore they were headed to land.

Life Bread

MATTHEW 14:34–36
MARK 6:53–56
JOHN 6:22–59

The next day, the crowd that stayed on the other side of the sea realized that there had been only one small boat and that Jesus had not gone into it with His disciples—they had gone away by themselves. By now some boats from Tiberias had come near where they had eaten the bread blessed by the Lord. When the crowd realized He and His disciples were gone, they got into the boats and came to Capernaum looking for Jesus.

When they had crossed to the other side, Jesus and His disciples landed at Gennesaret and anchored at the shore. As soon as they got out of the boat, the men of that place recognized Him. When the people heard that He was back from the other side of the sea, they asked, "Rabbi, when did You get here?" Jesus answered, "I tell you the truth, you have been searching for Me not because you saw the miracles but because I fed you the loaves and it filled you." They ran and sent out word through the countryside; they brought Him all who were sick on mats to His location.

Wherever He went—village, town, or countryside—they laid their sick in the marketplace and begged Him to let them touch the edge of His cloak. Whoever touched Him was healed and restored to health.

Jesus said, "Stop working for food that perishes. Work for the food that lasts to eternal life, which the Son of Man provides you. God the Father has placed His seal of approval on Him."

To that they said, "What are we to do to habitually perform the works of God?"

Jesus answered, "The work of God is to believe in the One Whom He has sent to you."

Therefore, they answered, "What miracle will You perform so that we may see it and believe You? What work will You perform? Our forefathers ate the manna in the wilderness. The Scriptures say, 'He gave them bread from heaven to eat.'"

Jesus responded, saying, "I tell you the truth, it is not that Moses gave you bread from heaven, but it is My Father Who gives you the true Bread from heaven. The Bread of God is He Who comes down out of heaven and gives life to the world."

Then they said, "Lord, give us this bread, now and forever!"

Jesus replied, "I am the Bread of Life. He who comes to Me will never hunger or thirst any more. Nevertheless, as I told you, although you have seen, you do not really believe in Me. Every person the Father has entrusted to Me eventually comes to Me. Once that person comes to Me, I will never reject him. I did not come down from heaven to follow My own will. I came to accomplish the will of Him Who sent Me. The will of the Father Who sent Me is that I not lose any of those He has given Me but raise them all up at the last day. The will of My Father is that everyone who sees the Son and believes in Him will have eternal life, and I will raise them up at the last day."

At this, because He said, "I am the Bread that came down from heaven," the Jews began to grumble and argue over Him, saying, "Is not this Jesus, Joseph's Son, Whose father and mother we know? How can He now say, 'I came down out of heaven'?"

Jesus said, "Stop grumbling among yourselves. No one can come to Me unless the Father Who sent Me gives him the desire to come to Me. Then I will raise him from the dead at the last day. This is what the prophets meant when they wrote, 'They will all be taught by God.' Anyone who has listened and learned from the Father comes to Me. No one has seen the Father except the One Who comes from the Father—only He has seen the Father. I tell you the truth, whoever believes in Me possesses eternal life—I am the Bread of Life. Your ancestors ate manna in the desert and died, but this is the Bread that comes down from heaven—anyone eating this Bread will not die. I am the Living Bread Who came down from heaven. Anyone who eats this Bread will live forever. The Bread is My flesh that I give to the world for life."

Then the Jews started to angrily fight among themselves, saying, "How can this Man give us His flesh to eat?"

Jesus said to them, "I tell you the truth, you cannot have life in you unless you eat the flesh of the Son of Man and drink His blood. Whoever eats My flesh and drinks My blood possesses eternal life, and I will raise him up from the dead on the last day. My flesh is real food and My blood is real drink. Whoever eats My flesh and drinks My blood dwells continually in Me and I in him. Just as the living Father sent Me and I live because of the Father, so he who takes Me for his food will live because of Me. This is the Bread that came down from heaven. It is not like the manna that your ancestors ate and yet died. Whoever feeds on this Bread will live forever." He said these things while teaching in the synagogue in Capernaum.

Difficult Teaching

JOHN 6:60–71

Many of His disciples heard this and said, "This is difficult. Who can be expected to accept it?"

Jesus knew that His disciples were grumbling about this and said, "Does this offend you and cause you to stumble? What would be your reaction if you saw the Son of Man ascending to where He came from? The Spirit gives life. The flesh is of no benefit. The truths I have spoken to are spirit and life. However, some of you fail to believe." Jesus knew from the start who did not believe and who would betray Him. He went on to say, "This is why I told you that no one can come to Me on his own unless he is enabled to do so by the Father."

As a result of this, many of His disciples left—they no longer wanted to be associated with Him. Then Jesus said to the Twelve, "Do you also desire to go away and leave Me?" Peter replied, "Lord, to whom shall we go? You have the words of eternal life. We know that You are the Christ, the Holy One of God." Jesus responded, "Did I not choose you, the Twelve? Yet one of you is the devil!" He was referring to Judas, son of Simon Iscariot. This man, though one of the Twelve, was even then about to betray Him.

Polluted Heart

MATTHEW 15:1–20
MARK 7:1–23

Then some Pharisees and religion experts came to Jesus from Jerusalem and gathered around Him. They had seen that some of His disciples ate with unwashed hands. The Pharisees and Jews in general never eat without going through the motions of the hand-washing tradition of their ancestors. When they come from the marketplace, they do not eat unless they wash themselves. Additionally, they faithfully observe many other traditions, such as washing cups, pitchers, and pots. The Pharisees and religion experts asked Jesus, "Why do Your disciples violate the traditions of the elders and eat without washing their hands?"

Jesus replied, "Why do you violate the commandments of God for the sake of your tradition? You disregard the commandment of God and cling to the traditions of men. God, through Moses, said, 'Honor your father and mother,' and, 'Anyone who speaks evil of his father or mother should be put to death.' However, you say, 'A man is exempt if he says to his father or mother that any help you might have received from me is Corban—a gift already given as an offering to God.' Then you no longer permit him to do anything for his father or mother—you nullify God's Word for the sake of your traditions. You do a lot of things like this. Hypocrites! Isaiah's prophecy was right when he said,

> These people honor Me with their lips,
>> but their heart is far away from Me.
> Their worship of Me is useless;
>> they teach as doctrine the rules of men."

Jesus then called the crowd to Him again and said, "Listen to Me, everyone, and understand. It is not what goes into a man's mouth from outside a man that pollutes him. Instead, it is what comes out of a man's mouth that pollutes him."

Then His disciples came and asked Him, "Did You know how displeased the Pharisees were when they heard what You said?"

Jesus answered, "Every plant that was not planted by My heavenly Father will be pulled up by the roots. Disregard them; they are blind teachers. If a blind man leads a blind man, both will fall in the ditch."

When He had left the crowd and had entered the house, His disciples said to Him through Peter, "Explain this parable to us."

Jesus replied, "Do you also lack understanding? Do you not see that anything that goes into your mouth from the outside goes into the stomach and then is eliminated from the body? This does not pollute you. It does not reach your heart but only the digestive tract where it is passed out of the body." (Consequently, Jesus declared all food clean.) He continued: "What comes out of a man's mouth comes from the heart—this is what pollutes him. From the heart come evil thoughts, sexual immorality, murder, adultery, theft, greed, malice, deceit, indecent conduct, envy, slander, pride, foolishness, fornication, lies, and irreverent speech. These evil things come from within your heart and are the source of your pollution. Eating or not eating certain foods—washing or not washing your hands—does not pollute you."

Dogs Fed

MATTHEW 15:21–31
MARK 7:24–37

Jesus departed from there and withdrew to the vicinity of Tyre and Sidon. He entered a house there and did not want anyone to know it; nonetheless, it was not possible for Him to escape notice. Instead, they had hardly arrived and immediately a Canaanite woman, who had a demon-possessed little daughter, heard where He was, came from that vicinity, and fell at His feet. The woman was Greek, Syro-Phoenician by race. She begged Him to drive the demon out of her little daughter, saying, "Have mercy on me, Lord, Son of David! Mercy, Master, Son of David! My daughter is cruelly afflicted by a demon."

When Jesus ignored her, His disciples came and implored Him, "Send her away. She keeps shouting out after us."

Jesus answered, "I was sent only to the sheep of the house of Israel."

However, the woman came back to Jesus, knelt before Him in worship, and said, "Lord, help me!"

Jesus replied, "First let the children be fed, because it is not right to take the children's bread and throw it to the dogs."

She said, "Yes, Lord, but even the dogs under the table get crumbs dropped by the children from the master's table."

Then Jesus said to her, "Woman, your faith is great! Your request is granted as you wish because of this response; go home. The demon has permanently left your daughter." Her daughter immediately became well—she went home and found her child lying on the bed. The demon was gone for good.

Jesus departed from there and walked along the shore of the Sea of Galilee. Then He climbed a mountain and sat there, ready to receive visitors. Large crowds came to Him, bringing the lame, crippled, blind, and mute plus many others. They laid them at the feet of Jesus and He healed them. The people were amazed when they saw the mutes speaking, the crippled healthy, the lame walking around, and the blind able to see. They praised the God of Israel.

Then He left the region of Tyre, went through Sidon to the Sea of Galilee and into the region of Decapolis. Some people brought to Him a man who could not hear and had difficulty speaking. They begged Jesus to place His hand on him. He took the man off by himself away from the crowd, put His fingers in the man's ears, spit, and put it on the man's tongue. Then Jesus looked up to heaven and, with a deep sigh, said, "*Ephphatha!*"—which means, "Open up!" At this, the man could hear; the impediment to his tongue was removed and he began speaking distinctly.

Jesus commanded them not to tell anyone, but the more He did so the more widely they talked about it. They were utterly amazed and said, "He has done everything well. He even makes the deaf hear and the mute speak."

Four Thousand

MATTHEW 15:32–39
MARK 8:1–10

In those days, again a large crowd gathered and they had nothing to eat. Jesus called His disciples to Him and said, "I feel pity for these people because they have been with Me for three days and now they have nothing left to eat. I am not willing to send them away hungry lest they faint on the way. Some of them have come a long distance."

His disciples replied, "Where in this desolate place would we get enough bread to feed this large crowd?"

Jesus asked, "How many loaves of bread do you have?"

"Seven loaves," they said, "plus a few small fish." Jesus directed the crown of people to sit down on the ground. After giving thanks, He took the seven loaves of bread, broke them, and kept on giving them to His disciples so they could serve the crowd—they served the people. Then He gave thanks for the few small fish and told His disciples to distribute them as well to the people. They all ate and were satisfied. When they finished eating, the disciples gathered seven large baskets of the broken pieces that were left. There were about four thousand men who ate, not including women and children. Then Jesus dismissed the crowd, got into the boat with His disciples, and went to the district of Damanoutha—they went to the coasts of Magadan.

Bad Yeast

MATTHEW 16:1–12
MARK 8:11–26

The Pharisees and Sadducees came and began to question and argue with Jesus. They tested Him by asking Him to show them a miracle as a sign from heaven to prove His divine authority. He sighed deeply in His spirit and said, "When evening comes you say, 'Red sky at night, sailor's delight; red sky at morning, sailors take warning.' You know how to interpret the appearance of the sky but you cannot interpret the signs of the times. A wicked and morally unfaithful generation craves for a sign. Why does this generation seek a miraculous sign? I tell you the truth, no sign will be given to this generation except the sign of Jonah." Then He left them and went away—He got into the boat and again crossed to the other side.

On their way across the lake, the disciples discovered they had forgotten to bring any bread except for a single loaf they had in the boat. Jesus warned them, "Be careful. Watch out for the yeast of the Pharisees, Sadducees, and the followers of Herod."

The disciples discussed this with each other and said, "It is because we have no bread—we forgot it." Jesus was aware of their discussion and asked, "You men of little faith, why are you worried about the fact that you have no bread? Do you still not understand? Do you have hard hearts? Do you have unseeing eyes and unhearing ears? Do you not remember the five loaves of bread I broke for the five thousand? How many baskets of leftover fragments did you pick up?" They replied, "Twelve." Jesus continued: "Do you not remember the seven loaves that fed four thousand? How many baskets of leftovers did you collect?" They answered, "Seven." He said, "Do you not yet understand? How is it that you fail to understand I was not talking to you about bread? Be on alert to the yeast of the Pharisees and Sadducees." Then they understood He was not talking about the yeast of bread but to beware of the teaching of the Pharisees and Sadducees.

They came to Bethsaida and some people brought to Him a blind man and begged Jesus to touch him. Taking him by the hand, He led him out of the village. When He put spit on the man's eyes and laid hands on him, He asked him, "Do you see anything?"

He looked up and said, "I see people, but they look like walking trees." Once again, Jesus put His hands on the man's eyes. The man looked intently and his sight was restored perfectly—he saw everything clearly. Jesus sent him home, saying, "Do not go into the town or tell anyone."

God's Christ

MATTHEW 16:13–20
MARK 8:27–30
LUKE 9:18–21

When Jesus and His disciples went on and came to the towns of the region around Caesarea Philippi, there was a time He was praying privately with His disciples nearby. As they walked, He asked them, "Who do the crowds of people say the Son of Man is? Who do the people say I am?"

They replied, "Some say John the Baptist, others say Elijah, and still others say Jeremiah or one of the other prophets from long ago who has come back to life."

Jesus pressed them and asked, "What about you, who do you say I am?"

Simon Peter replied, "You are the Christ of God, the Son of the living God."

Jesus responded, "Blessed are you, Simon, son of Jonah. Men did not reveal this to you; My Father in heaven revealed it to you. I tell you that you are Peter and on this rock I will build My church. The gates of hell will not be able to overpower it. I will give you the keys of heaven. Whatever you declare unlawful on earth will be unlawful in heaven and whatever you declare lawful on earth will be lawful in heaven."

Then Jesus warned His disciples not to tell this to anyone—He warned them not to tell anyone that He was Jesus the Christ.

Peter Rebuked

MATTHEW 16:21–28
MARK 8:31–9:1
LUKE 9:22–27

From that time on, Jesus made it clear to His disciples by teaching them, saying, "It is necessary that the Son of Man must go to Jerusalem, suffer many things, and be rejected by the elders, high priests, and religion experts, be killed, and after three days be raised up alive." He said this plainly and explicitly to them. Peter took Him aside and began to rebuke Him sharply, saying, "God forbid it, Lord! This shall never happen to You!"

However, Jesus, turning and looking at His disciples, rebuked Peter, saying, "Get behind Me, Satan! You are a hindrance to Me. You are not setting your mind on the things of God but on the interests of man. You have no idea how God works."

Then Jesus called to Him the crowds along with the disciples and said to them all, "If anyone intends to be My disciple, he must deny himself, take up his cross and follow Me. Whoever wants to save his earthly life will lose eternal life, but whoever loses his earthly life for My sake and the Gospel will find everlasting life. What profit will it be for a man if he gains the whole world and forfeits his life in God's kingdom? What can a man exchange for his soul's life in God's kingdom? Whoever is ashamed of Me and My words in this adulterous and sinful generation, the Son of Man will be ashamed of him when He comes in the glory of His Father with the holy angels—then He will reward everyone according to his deeds. I tell you the truth, some who are standing here will not taste death before they see the Son of Man coming in His kingdom."

Jesus' Transfiguration

MATTHEW 17:1–13
MARK 9:2–13
LUKE 9:28–36

About eight days after these teachings (six days between Peter's confession and the transfiguration), Jesus took Peter and the brothers, James and John, with Him and led them up a high mountain by themselves to pray. As He was praying, He was transfigured before them—His face shone like the sun and His clothes became dazzling white as light, whiter than anyone could bleach them. Just then, two men, Moses and Elijah, appeared in glorious splendor, speaking with Him about His departure from His earthly life, which He was about to complete at Jerusalem.

Peter and those with him were very sleepy. When they were fully awake, they saw Jesus in His glory and the two men standing with Him. When Moses and Elijah were leaving, Peter said, "Master, Lord, Rabbi, it is good for us to be here. If You approve, we will build three shelters—one for You, one for Moses, and one for Elijah." (He did not know what he was saying—they were very afraid.)

Then, while he was still speaking, a bright cloud appeared and overshadowed them. They were seized with fear as they entered the cloud. A voice came from the cloud, saying, "This is My Son Whom I have chosen and love. I am greatly pleased with Him. Listen to Him!"

When the disciples heard it, they fell on their faces and were struck with fear. Suddenly, when the sound of the voice died away and when they looked up, they saw no one except Jesus; He was alone—they no longer saw anyone with them except Jesus. He came over, touched them, and said, "Get up and do not be afraid."

As they were coming down the mountain, Jesus commanded them, saying, "Do not mention to anyone what you saw here until after the Son of Man is raised from the dead." The disciples kept this matter to themselves, discussing with each other what "raised from the dead" meant. They told no one, at that time, what they had seen this day.

Jesus' disciples asked Him, "Why do the religion experts say that Elijah must come first?"

Jesus replied, "I tell you, Elijah does come first and restore all things. Why, then, must the Son of Man suffer at their hands? According to Scripture, He will be rejected and suffer many things. I tell you, Elijah has already come, but they did not recognize him and they did whatever they desired to do to him." Then the disciples understood He was talking about John the Baptist.

Kernel Faith

MATTHEW 17:14–23
MARK 9:14–32
LUKE 9:37–45

The next day, when they came down from the mountain to the other disciples, they approached and saw a large crowd around them and the religion experts with them. Immediately, the entire crowd, when they saw Jesus, was amazed at His appearance—He still glowed from the transfiguration—and ran to meet Him. Jesus asked, "What are you arguing about with them?" As they approached, a man came out of the crowd and knelt before Jesus, saying, "Master, Teacher, I brought to You my son who is possessed with a demon that makes him mute. I beg You to look at him; he is my only son. Have mercy on him. He has seizures, goes out of his mind, and suffers greatly. Whenever the demon seizes him, he suddenly screams and it throws him into convulsions to the ground. He foams at the mouth, grinds his teeth, and goes motionless. It beats him and seldom leaves him alone. He frequently falls into the fire or into the water. I brought him to Your disciples and asked them to drive out the demon, but they could not help him."

Jesus replied, "O unbelieving and perverse generation, how long shall I stay and bear with you? Bring the boy, your son, to Me." So they brought the boy to Him. When the demon saw Jesus, it immediately threw him to the ground in a convulsion—the boy fell to the ground and rolled around, foaming at the mouth. Jesus asked the boy's father, "How long has he been like this?" The father replied, "Ever since he was a little boy. It often throws him into fire or water to kill him. If you can do anything, have pity on us and help us!" Jesus said, "You say to Me, 'If You can help us.' All things are possible to him who believes." At once, the father of the boy cried out, saying, "Lord, I do believe; help me overcome my unbelief!" When Jesus noticed a crowd was rapidly gathering, He rebuked the demon, saying, "You dumb and deaf demon, I command you to come out of him and never enter him again." After crying out, the demon convulsed the boy violently and came out. The boy looked like a corpse so much that many said, "He is dead." However, Jesus took him by the hand and lifted him up—the boy stood, healed from that moment. Jesus then gave the boy back to his father. The crowd was astounded at the greatness of God.

When Jesus had gone indoors, His disciples asked Him privately, "Why could we not drive the demon out?"

Jesus answered, "This kind can be driven out only by prayer, and you have little faith. I tell you the truth, if you have faith as little as a mustard seed, you can say to this mountain, 'Move from here to that place over there,' and it will move. Nothing will be impossible to you."

When they left that place and were passing through Galilee (He did not want anyone to know where they were because He was teaching His disciples), while everyone was amazed at what He was doing among them, Jesus said to His disciples, "Let these words sink in: The Son of Man is going to be betrayed into the hands of ungodly men; they will kill Him and He will be raised alive again on the third day." However, they did not comprehend what He meant and were afraid to ask Him what He meant. It was concealed from them so that they did not grasp its meaning. The disciples felt deep grief.

Paying Taxes

MATTHEW 17:24–27

When they arrived in Capernaum, the tax men who collected the temple tax came to Peter and asked, "Does your Teacher pay the temple tax?"

Peter replied, "Yes, of course."

When he came into the house, Jesus was the first to speak to him about it and asked, "What do you think, Simon? From whom do the earthly kings collect duty and taxes? Do they collect it from their family or from others?"

Peter answered, "From others."

Jesus said, "Then the family is exempt. However, so we do not offend them, go and throw in a hook into the lake. Take the first fish that comes up. When you open its mouth, you will find a coin. Take it and give it to them to pay the temple tax for Me and yourself."

First Place

MATTHEW 18:1–9
MARK 9:33–50
LUKE 9:46–50

At the same time, they arrived at Capernaum. When they were in the house, He asked them, "What were you discussing and arguing about on the road?" However, they kept silent because they had been disputing with one another about who among them was greatest and who would be most famous. Then the disciples came to Jesus and asked, "Who is the greatest in the kingdom of heaven?"

Jesus sat down and called the Twelve—He knew what they were thinking from their hearts. Then He said, "If anyone desires to be first, he must take the last place and be the servant of all." To continue His answer, He called over a little child and put him at His side to stand among them. Taking him in His arms, He said to them, "I tell you the truth, unless you repent and become like little children, you can never enter the kingdom of heaven. Therefore, whoever humbles himself like this child is greatest in the kingdom of heaven. Moreover, whoever receives one little child like this in My name accepts Me; whoever accepts Me receives the One Who sent Me. He who is lowliest among you is truly great."

John said to Him, "Teacher, Master, we saw a man driving out demons using Your name, and we forbade him because he was not one of our group."

Jesus said, "Do not forbid him. No one who can perform a miracle using My name can turn around and say something evil of Me. Whoever is not against us is for us. I tell you the truth, anyone who gives you a cup of water to drink because you belong to and bear the name of Christ will not lose his reward.

"On the other hand, if anyone causes one of these little ones who believe in Me to sin, it would be more expedient for him to have a heavy millstone hung around his neck and be thrown into the depths of the sea to drown. Woe to the world because of the temptations that cause people to sin. Temptations are inevitable, but woe to the man through whom the temptation comes!

"If your hand or your foot causes you to sin, cut it off and throw it away. It is better to live your life maimed or lame than to have two hands, and two feet, and be cast into eternal fire. If your eye causes you to sin, pluck it out and throw it away. It is better to live your life with one eye than to have two eyes and be cast into eternal fire, where the worm does not die and the fire is not put out.

"Everyone will be salted with fire. Salt is beneficial. If it loses its saltiness, how will you make it salty again? Have salt in yourselves and be at peace with one another."

Chapter 5

GOING TOWARD JERUSALEM

Disbelieving Brothers

JOHN 7:1–9

After these things, Jesus walked around in Galilee. He was unwilling to travel in Judea because the Jews there sought to kill Him. In spite of this, when the Feast of Tabernacles was drawing near, his brothers said to Him, "Leave here and go to Judea so Your disciples there can also see Your miracles. No one who desires to be known publicly does things secretly. If You do these things, You must show Yourself to the world." They said this because even His own brothers did not believe in Him.

Then Jesus said to them, "My time has not yet come, but any time is suitable for you. The world cannot be expected to hate you, but it hates Me because I expose its evil deeds. Go to the feast by yourselves, because it is not the right time for Me!" Having said this, He remained behind in Galilee.

The Christ?

JOHN 7:10–52

However, after His brothers had gone up to the Feast, He also went, but in secret and not publicly to prevent drawing attention to Himself.

As a result, the Jews were looking for Him and asking, "Where is that Man?"

There was a lot of whispered discussion about Him among the crowds. Some were saying, "He is a good man." Others were saying, "He deceives the people and leads them astray." Yet, no one dared to say anything publicly about Him because they feared the Jewish leaders.

Not until the Feast was half over did Jesus go up to the temple courts to teach. The Jews were impressed and said, "How did this Man get so much knowledge without having studied in formal education?"

Jesus answered them, saying, "My teaching is not My own. It comes from Him Who sent Me. If any man desires to do the will of God, he will discover whether My teaching comes from God or whether I speak on My own authority. He who speaks on his own authority seeks honor for himself, but he who seeks the glory of the one who sent him is trustworthy. Did not Moses give you the law? Yet none of you keeps the law. If that is true, why are you trying to kill Me?"

The crowd said, "You are possessed by a demon! Who is trying to kill You?"

Jesus answered them, saying, "I did one miracle and you all were astonished at it. Now, because Moses established circumcision among you—it did not originate from Moses but from the patriarchs—all of you perform it even on the Sabbath. If to avoid breaking the law you circumcise on the Sabbath, why are you angry with Me for healing a man's entire body on the Sabbath? Stop judging according to appearances and judge rightly."

Then some of the people of Jerusalem said, "Is not this the Man they were seeking to kill? He is speaking openly in public and they are not saying anything to Him to stop Him. Is it possible the leaders know He is the Christ? Yet we know from where this Man came; when the Christ comes, nobody will know from where He comes."

Then Jesus cried out as He was teaching in the temple, saying, "Yes, you think you know Me and from where I came. I have not come on My own authority, but He Who sent Me is real and you do not know Him. I come from Him—that is how I know Him. He personally sent Me."

At this they tried to arrest Him, but nobody laid a hand on Him because His time had not yet come. Many from the crowd believed in Him, saying, "When the Christ comes, can we expect Him to provide more miracles than those done by this Man?"

When the Pharisees heard the crowd murmuring these things about Jesus, the chief priests and Pharisees sent temple guards to arrest Him.

Jesus, therefore, said, "I will only be with you a little while longer and then I will return to the One Who sent Me. You will look for Me but be unable to find Me—where I am you cannot come."

Then the Jews said to one another, "Where does this Man intend to go that we will not be able to find Him? Will He go to the Jews dispersed among the Greeks to teach them? What did He mean by the statement when He said, 'You will look for Me but be unable to find Me,' and, 'Where I am you cannot come'?"

On the final and most important day of the Feast, Jesus stood and cried in a loud voice, saying, "If any man is thirsty, let him come to Me and drink. If you believe in Me, rivers of living water will continuously flow, as it says in Scripture." (He was speaking of the Spirit, Whom those who believed in Him were going to receive—the Spirit had not yet been given because Jesus had not yet been glorified.)

Some of the crowd who heard these words said, "This man is certainly the Prophet." Others said, "He is the Christ." Still others were asking, "Surely the Christ does not come from Galilee, does He? Does not the Scripture inform us that the Christ will come from the offspring of David and from Bethlehem, the town where David lived?" So there arose a division among the people because of Him. Some of them wanted to arrest Him, but no one laid a hand on Him.

As a result, the temple guards went to the chief priests and Pharisees, who said to them, "Why did you not bring Him here with you?" The guards replied, "No mere man ever spoke the way He speaks." The Pharisees said, "Have you also been led astray? Not a single person in authority or Pharisee believes in Him, do they? This rabble does not know the law—there is a curse on them."

Then Nicodemus, the man who had come to Jesus earlier and was one of them, asked, "Our law does not convict anyone without first listening to him and finding out what he is doing, does it?" They replied, "Are you also from Galilee? Examine the Scriptures and you will see that no prophet rises to prominence from Galilee."

Sinful Accusers

JOHN 7:53—8:11

Then everyone went to his own home, but Jesus went to the Mount of Olives. At dawn, He came back into the temple again and the people came to Him. He sat down and taught them.

The religion experts and the Pharisees brought in a woman who had been caught in an act of adultery. They made her stand in the middle of them and said, "Teacher, this woman was caught in the act of adultery. Moses, in the law, commanded us to stone such women. What do You say to do with her?" They said this to trap Him in the hope of finding grounds to accuse Him.

However, Jesus bent down and wrote on the ground with His finger. When they persisted with their question, He straightened up and said to them, "The one among you who is sinless, go first. Throw the stone." Bending down again, He wrote some more on the ground.

Hearing that, they began to walk away, conscience stricken, beginning with the oldest, until Jesus was left alone with the woman, who was still standing before Him. Jesus stood up and asked her, "Woman, where are they? Does no one condemn you?"

She replied, "No one, Lord."

Then Jesus said, "Neither do I condemn you. Go on your way. From now on, sin no more."

Not Alone

JOHN 8:12–30

Jesus once again spoke to the people, saying, "I am the Light of the world. Whoever follows Me will not walk in the dark but will have the Light of life."

Therefore, the Pharisees said to Him, "You are testifying on behalf of Yourself; Your testimony is invalid."

Jesus replied, "Even if I testify for Myself, My testimony is valid—I know where I came from and where I am going to next. On the other hand, you do not know where I came from and where I am going to next. You judge according to what you can see and touch, but I am not judging anyone. If I do judge, My decisions are valid because I am not alone in making them. There are two of Us judging—I and the Father Who sent Me. Your own law states the testimonial evidence of two is reliable. I am One of the Two bearing witness of Myself, and the Other witness is the Father Who sent Me."

They said, "Where is Your Father?"

Jesus replied, "You neither know Me nor My Father. If you knew Me you also would know My Father." He said these things in the treasury while teaching in the temple. No one tried to arrest Him because it was not His time.

Once again Jesus said to them, "I am going away and you will look for Me, but you will die in your sin. It is not possible for you to come where I am going to go."

This caused the Jews to ask among themselves, saying, "Is He going to kill Himself? Is that what He means by saying, 'It is not possible for you to come where I am going to'?"

Jesus said to them, "You are from below; I am from above. You are of this world; I am not of this world. That is why I told you that you would die in your sins. If you do not believe I am Who I claim to be, then you will die in your sins."

Then they asked Him, "Who are You anyway?"

Jesus replied, "I am exactly what I have been claiming from the start. I have many things to say in judgment of you. He Who sent Me is reliable, and I only tell the world the things I have heard from Him."

They did not realize that He was speaking to them about the Father. So Jesus added, "When you raise up the Son of Man, then you will know Who I am—He for Whom you look—and that I do nothing of My own initiative or authority, but I speak only the things the Father taught Me. The One who sent Me is always with Me—My Father has not left Me alone because I always do what pleases Him." As Jesus spoke these things, many believed in Him.

God's Children

JOHN 8:31–47

Then Jesus said to the Jews who believed in Him, "If you hold fast to My teaching, then you are truly My disciples. You will know the truth and the truth will make you free."

They said to Him, "We are descendants of Abraham and have never been slaves to anyone. What do You mean when You say, 'The truth will make you free'?"

Jesus replied, "I tell you the truth, anyone who practices sin is the slave of sin. A slave has no permanent place in the family household, but the son of the house belongs to it forever. So if the Son liberates you, then you are indeed free. I know you are descended from Abraham; however, you plan to kill Me because My teaching does not find a place in you. I tell you things I have seen in My Father's presence, and your actions show what you have learned from your father."

They retorted, "Our father is Abraham!"

Jesus said, "If you were truly Abraham's children, then you would follow his example. Instead, you are seeking to kill Me, a Man Who has told to you the truth that I heard from God. Abraham never did that sort of thing—you do the works of your father."

They said, "We are not illegitimate children. We have one Father, God."

Jesus said to them, "If God was your father, you would love Me because I came from the presence of God. I did not even come on My own accord—God sent Me. Why can you not understand one word I say? It is because you are unable to hear My teaching because you do not want to listen. You are like your father, the Devil, and all you want to do is please him. He was a murderer from the very start. He does not tolerate the truth because there is not a shred of truth in him. When he lies he speaks what is natural to him because he is a liar and the father of all lies. Nevertheless, because I tell you the truth, you do not believe Me. Can any one of you convict Me of any wrongdoing or convict Me of any sin? If I speak the truth, why do you not believe Me? Those who belong to God hear what He says. The reason you do not listen to Me is because you do not belong to God."

I Am

JOHN 8:48–59

The Jews then said, "Are we not right in saying You are a Samaritan and You are possessed by a demon?"

Jesus said, "I am not possessed by a demon. However, I honor My Father and you dishonor Me. I do not seek honor for Myself, but there is One Who seeks it and He is the Judge. I tell you the truth, if anyone lives in accordance with My teaching, he will never taste death."

Then the Jews said to Him, "Now we know You are possessed by a demon. Abraham died, the prophets died, and You say, 'If anyone lives in accordance with My teaching, he will never taste death.' Are You greater than our father Abraham? He died and so did the prophets. Who do You think You are?"

Jesus said, "If I honor Myself, it would be worthless. My Father, the One you say is your God, is the One Who honors Me. Yet you do not recognize Him but I do recognize Him. If I said that I do not recognize

Him, I would be like you—a liar. Nonetheless, I do recognize Him and I obey His teaching. Your father Abraham rejoiced at the prospect of seeing My day—he did see it and was glad."

The Jews said to Him, "You are not yet fifty years old and You have seen Abraham?"

"I tell you the truth," said Jesus, "I Am long before Abraham was born." So they picked up stones to throw at Him but Jesus hid Himself in the crowd and left the temple.

Blind Man

JOHN 9:1–41

As Jesus walked along, He saw a man blind from birth. His disciples asked Him, "Rabbi, who sinned, this man or his parents, causing him to be born blind?"

Jesus answered, "Neither this man nor his parents sinned, but he was born blind so that the work of God would be displayed in him. We must do the work of Him Who sent Me while it is daylight. Night is coming when no man can work. As long as I am in the world, I am the Light of the world."

When He finished saying this, He spat on the ground, made mud with His saliva, and put it on the man's eyes. Then He said, "Go and wash in the Pool of Siloam" (which means Sent). So the man went away, washed, and came back being able to see.

Then his neighbors and those who had previously seen him as a beggar said, "Is this not the man who used to sit and beg?" Some said, "He is that man." Others said, "No, it is not the same man at all—he just looks a lot like him." However, he said, "I am the man."

They said, "How were your eyes opened up?"

He replied, "A Man named Jesus made some mud and rubbed it on my eyes. He told me, 'Go and wash in the Pool of Siloam.' I did what He said. When I washed, I could see."

They asked, "So where is He?"

He replied, "I do not know."

They brought the man who was formerly blind to the Pharisees. The day when Jesus made the mud and healed his blindness was the Sabbath. Therefore, the Pharisees asked him again how he received his sight. He said, "He put mud on my eyes, I washed, and now I see."

Some of the Pharisees said, "This Man cannot be from God because He does not observe the Sabbath."

Nevertheless, others said, "How can a man who is a sinner perform miracles?" So there was a difference of opinion among them.

They said to the blind man again, "What do you say about Him since He opened your eyes?"

He replied, "He is a prophet."

Still the Jews did not believe the man had been blind until they summoned the man's parents. They asked them, "Is this your son, the one you say was born blind? How is it that he now sees?"

His parents said, "We know he is our son and we know he was born blind. However, we do not know how he can see now or who restored his sight. Ask him. He is old enough to speak for himself." His parents were talking like this because they feared the Jews, who had already agreed that anyone who acknowledged Jesus to be the Christ would be put out of the synagogue. That is why his parents said, "Ask him. He is old enough to speak for himself."

So a second time they summoned the man who had been blind and said to him, "Give praise to God. We know this Man is a sinner."

He replied, "Whether He is a sinner or not, I do not know. One thing I do know is that I once was blind but now I see."

They said, "What did He do to you? How did He open your eyes?"

He replied, "I already told you and you did not listen. Why do you want to hear it again? Do you want to become His disciple, too?"

With that they insulted him, saying, "You are a disciple of this Man but we are disciples of Moses. We know for certain that God spoke to Moses, but as for the Fellow, we have no idea from where He came."

The man answered, "Well, this is amazing! He healed my eyes and you do not know from where He comes! We know that God does not listen to sinners, but He does listen to anyone who worships Him and does His will. Since the beginning of time it has never been heard of anyone restoring the sight of a man born blind. If this Man did not come from God, He would not be able to do anything like this miracle."

They said to him, "You were born totally in sin and you dare to teach us?" So they threw him out of the synagogue.

Jesus heard that they had thrown him out, and upon finding him, He said, "Do you believe in the Son of Man?"

The man said, "Point Him out to me, Sir, so that I can believe in Him."

Jesus said, "You have seen Him. In fact, He is talking to you right now."

"Lord, I believe," the man said and worshiped Him.

Jesus then said, "For judgment I came into the world so that the sightless may see and so that those who pretend to see may become blind."

Some Pharisees overheard Him and said, "Does that mean You are calling us blind?"

Jesus said, "If you were blind, you would be blameless of sin, but since you claim to see everything clearly, your sin remains and you are guilty."

Good Shepherd

JOHN 10:1–21

Jesus continued, saying, "I tell you the truth, if a man does not enter in a sheep pen by the door but climbs in some other way, he is a thief and a robber. He who enters by the door is the shepherd of the sheep. To him the watchman opens the door; the sheep heed his voice. He calls his own sheep by name and leads them out. When he gets all his sheep outside, he walks in front of them and they follow him because they know his voice. They will never follow a stranger but will run away from him because they do not recognize the voice of strangers."

They did not understand what He was talking about when He used this parable. Consequently, He tried again and said, "I tell you the truth, I am the Door for the sheep. All the others who came before Me are thieves and robbers, but the true sheep did not obey them. I am the Door; whoever enters in through Me will be saved forever. He will freely come in and go out; he will find pasture. The thief only comes to steal, kill, and destroy. I came so they can have an abundant life that is full and overflows.

"I am the Good Shepherd. The Good Shepherd risks His own life for the sheep. A hired hand is neither the shepherd nor owner of the sheep. When he sees a wolf coming, he abandons the sheep and runs away. Then the wolf attacks and scatters the sheep. The hired hand flees because he only works for money and cares nothing for the sheep.

"I am the Good Shepherd. I know My own sheep and they know Me even as the Father knows Me and I know the Father. I am giving My own life on behalf of the sheep. Also, I have other sheep that are not of this fold. I must bring them, too. They will also heed My voice. Then there will be one flock under one Shepherd. This is why the Father loves Me: because I lay down My life so that I can take it up again. No one takes it from Me, but I lay it down voluntarily. I have the power to lay it down; I also have the power to take it up again. These are the instructions I received from My Father."

There arose a fresh division of opinion among the Jews because He said these things. Many of them said, "He has a demon possessing Him and is insane. Why do you listen to Him?" Others said, "These are not the things said by a man possessed by a demon. Can a demon open the eyes of the blind?"

Chapter 6

JESUS' TEACHING CONTINUES

Follow Me

MATTHEW 8:18–22
LUKE 9:51–62

When the time approached for His ascension, Jesus resolutely set His face to go toward Jerusalem. He sent messengers on ahead and they came to a Samaritan town to make arrangements for Him. However, they did not welcome Him because His face was set to head to Jerusalem. When the disciples James and John saw this, they said, "Lord, do You want us to command fire to come down and consume them like Elijah did?" Jesus turned and rebuked them, saying, "You do not know what kind of spirit you are, because the Son of Man did not come to destroy men's lives but to save them." Then they went to another town.

When Jesus saw the large crowds around Him, He gave orders to cross to the other side of the lake. As they were walking along the road, a religion expert came up to Him and said, "Teacher, I will follow You wherever You go."

Jesus replied, "Foxes have holes and birds of the air have nests, but the Son of Man has no place to lay His head."

Jesus said to another man, "Follow Me and become My disciple." The man replied, "Lord, allow me to first take care of my father until he dies."

However, Jesus said to him, "Follow Me and let the dead in sin bury their own dead, and make it your business to pursue life, not death, by proclaiming God's kingdom."

Then another said to Him, "I will follow You and become Your disciple, but first allow me to say goodbye to those at my home."

Jesus replied, "No one after putting his hand to the plow and then looking back is fit for God's kingdom."

Seventy Sent

MATTHEW 11:20–30
LUKE 10:1–24

After this the Lord appointed seventy others and sent them in pairs ahead of Him to every town and place where He intended to go. He said to them, "The harvest is indeed great but the laborers are few. Pray to the Lord of the harvest to send out laborers into His harvest. Go your ways. I am sending you out as lambs among wolves. Carry neither purse nor a provision bag nor a change of sandals. Do not slow down to greet anyone on the road.

"Whatever house you enter, first say, 'Peace to this house.' If anyone worthy of peace is there, your peace shall rest on him; if not, it shall come back to you. Stay in the same house, eating and drinking whatever they provide you—the laborer deserves his wages. Do not keep moving from house to house.

"When you enter a town and are welcomed, eat what they set before you. Heal anyone who is sick and tell them, 'God's kingdom has come close to you.' On the other hand, when you enter a town and are not welcomed, go out in the street and say, 'We wipe off against you even the dust of your town that sticks to our feet; yet understand this: God's kingdom has come close to you.' I say to you, it will be more tolerable in that day for Sodom than for that town."

Then Jesus began to denounce the cities in which He performed most of His miracles because they did not repent, saying, "Woe to you, Chorazin! Woe to you, Bethsaida! If the mighty miracles done in you had been performed in Tyre and Sidon, they would have repented long ago in sackcloth and ashes. I also tell you it shall be more tolerable for Tyre and Sidon on the day of judgment than for you. Capernaum, are you to be exalted to heaven? You shall be brought down to Hades because if the miracles performed in you had been done in Sodom, it would be here today. However, I tell you it shall be more tolerable for Sodom on the day of judgment than for you.

"The one who listens to you listens to Me. The one who rejects you rejects Me. Those who reject Me reject Him Who sent Me."

The seventy returned with joy, saying, "Lord, even the demons are subject to us in Your name."

Jesus said to them, "I know. I saw Satan fall from heaven like lightning. Behold, I have given you authority to trample upon snakes and scorpions, over all the power of the enemy—nothing will harm you. Nevertheless, do not rejoice that the spirits are subject to you—rejoice that your names are written in heaven."

At that, Jesus rejoiced in the Holy Spirit and said, "I thank You, Father, Lord of heaven and earth, because You have hidden these things from the wise and learned but revealed them to babies. Yes, Father, this was pleasing in Your sight—this was Your will.

"All these things have been entrusted to Me by My Father. No one fully understands the Son except the Father; no one fully understands the Father except the Son and anyone the Son chooses to reveal Him.

"Come to Me, all you who are weary and are burdened heavily; I will give you rest. Take My yoke upon you and walk with Me and work with Me—learn from Me; I am gentle and humble in heart—you will find rest for your souls. My yoke is easy and My burden is light."

Then, turning to His disciples, He said to them, "Blessed are the eyes that see the things you see. Many prophets and kings wanted to see what you are seeing but did not see them and to hear what you are hearing but did not hear them."

Samaritan Neighbor

LUKE 10:25–37

Then a certain religion expert stood up to try to test Jesus, saying, "Teacher, what do I need to do to inherit eternal life?"

Jesus answered, "What is written in the law? How do you interpret it?"

He replied, "That you love the Lord your God with all your heart, with all your soul, with all your strength, and with all your mind; also, love your neighbor as yourself."

Jesus said, "You have answered correctly. Do this and you will live endlessly in the kingdom of God."

Desiring to justify himself, he asked Jesus, "Who is my neighbor?"

Jesus answered by telling a story, saying, "A certain man was traveling from Jerusalem to Jericho. On the way he was attacked by robbers. They stripped him of his clothes, beat him up, and departed, leaving him half dead. By coincidence, a priest was going his way down the same road, but when he saw him, he passed on the other side. Then a Levite came to the place and also passed on the other side. However, when a Samaritan traveling the same road saw him, he was moved with pity for him. He went to him and bandaged his wounds, pouring on them oil and wine. Then he put him on his own beast, brought him to an inn, and took care of him. The morning of the next day, he took out two denarii" (two day's wages) "and gave them to the innkeeper, saying, 'Take care of him, and whatever more you spend, I will repay you when I return.'

"What do you think? Which of the three became a neighbor to the man attacked by robbers?"

The religion expert replied, "The one who showed mercy on him."

Jesus said to him, "Go and do likewise."

Mary's Choice

LUKE 10:38–42

It came to pass as they continued their travel, Jesus entered a certain town and a woman named Martha welcomed Him into her house. She had a sister named Mary who sat at Jesus' feet, listening to His teaching. However, Martha was distracted with the serving preparations. She came to Him and said, "Lord, do You not care that my sister has left me to do all the serving work? Tell her to help me!"

The Lord answered and said to her, "Martha, Martha, you are worried and troubled about many things, but only one thing is necessary; Mary has chosen it—the most advantageous part which will not be taken away from her."

Inner Cleanliness

LUKE 11:37–54

When He finished speaking, a Pharisee asked Him to have dinner with him. Jesus entered his house and sat right down at the table. The Pharisee noticed this and was astonished that Jesus did not first wash before the meal.

The Lord said to him, "You Pharisees clean the outside of the cup and plate, but your inside is full of greedy acts and wickedness. Stupid Pharisees! Did not He Who made the outside also make the inside? Dedicate your inner self and give generously to the poor; then all things are clean for you.

"Woe to you Pharisees! You tithe mint, rue, and all kinds of herbs from your gardens, but you disregard justice and the love of God. These things you should have done without leaving the others undone.

"Woe to you Pharisees! You love the best seats in the synagogues and respectful greetings in public places.

"Woe to you because you are like unmarked graves, and men unknowingly walk over them!"

One of the religion experts said, "Teacher, when You say these reproachful things, You also insult us."

Jesus replied, "Woe to you also, you religion experts! You load men down with burdens of rules and regulations that are hard to bear but never lift even a finger to help them.

"Woe to you! You build tombs for the prophets, and it was your ancestors who killed them. As a result, you bear witness and give your full approval for the deeds of your fathers because they killed them, and you build their tombs as monuments to them. For this reason, also, the wisdom of God said, 'I will send them prophets and apostles, some of whom they will kill and persecute.' Consequently, the blood of all the prophets, which was shed from the foundation of the world, is charged against this generation—they are responsible from the blood of Abel to the blood of Zechariah, who was slain between the altar and the sanctuary. Yes, I tell you, this generation is responsible for all of it.

"Woe to you religion experts! You have taken away the key to knowledge. You did not enter in yourselves and prevented those who were entering into knowledge."

As soon as Jesus left there, the religion experts and Pharisees became enraged and violently opposed Him—they besieged Him with questions to provoke Him on many subjects. They secretly plotted against Him to catch Him in something He might say.

Pharisee Leaven

LUKE 12:1–12

Meanwhile, when thousands of people had gathered together and were trampling on each other, Jesus began speaking to His disciples first, saying, "Be on your guard so you do not become contaminated with the leaven of the Pharisees, which is hypocrisy. Nothing is covered up that will not be revealed or hidden that will not be known! Therefore, whatever you have spoken in darkness shall be heard in the light, and that which you have whispered in the ear behind closed doors will be proclaimed from the housetops.

"I tell you, My friends, do not be afraid of those who can kill the body and after that can do nothing else. I will warn you of whom you should be afraid. Fear Him Who, after killing the body, has the power to throw you into hell. Yes, I say to you, fear Him. Are not sparrows sold for two pennies? Yet not one of them is forgotten by God. Even the very hairs of your head are all numbered. Therefore, do not fear, because you are more valuable than flocks of sparrows.

"I tell you, whoever acknowledges Me publicly before men, the Son of Man will also acknowledge him before God's angels. On the other hand, whoever rejects Me before men will be rejected before God's angels. Everyone who speaks a word against the Son of Man, he will be forgiven, but anyone who blasphemes against the Holy Spirit, it will not be forgiven him.

"When they bring you before their synagogues, rulers, and authorities, do not worry about how you will defend yourself or what you will say, because the Holy Spirit will give you the right words when the time comes."

Life Possessions

LUKE 12:13–21

Someone in the crowd said to Him, "Master, order my brother to divide the inheritance with me."

Jesus replied, "Man, who appointed Me judge and divider over you?" Then He said to the people, "Beware! Be on your guard against all forms of greed. A man's life does not consist of an abundance of possessions."

Then He told them a parable, saying, "The land of a certain rich man produced a plentiful crop. He thought to himself, 'What shall I do? I do not have enough room to store my crops.'

"Then he said, 'I will do this: I will tear down my barns and build bigger ones; there I will store all my crops and my goods.' Then I will say to my soul, 'Soul, you have many goods laid up for many years to come; take it easy, eat, drink, and be merry.'

"However, God said to him, 'You fool. This very night your soul will be required from you. Then who will own all your possessions?'

"So it is with anyone who hoards possessions for himself and is not rich in his relation to God."

Faithful Manager

LUKE 12:35–48

Jesus continued, saying to His disciples, "Be dressed ready to serve, and keep your lights burning. Be like servants waiting for their master to return from his wedding banquet, ready to open the door immediately when he arrives and knocks on the door. Blessed are those servants whom the master finds watching for him. I tell you the truth, he will dress himself to serve, have them recline at the table, and come to serve them. Blessed are servants whom the master finds ready whether he comes in the second or third watch of the night. Know that if the owner of the house knew what time the thief was coming, he would have been alert and would not have allowed a burglar to enter his house. You must also be ready, because the Son of Man comes at an hour you do not expect."

Peter said, "Lord, are You telling this parable just for us or is it for everybody?"

The Lord answered, "Who is the faithful and wise manager that the master will put in charge of his servants to feed them on time? Blessed is that servant whom the master finds doing his job when he arrives home. I tell you the truth, he will put him in charge of all his possessions. However, if the servant says to himself, 'My master delays in coming,' and begins beating the menservants and maidservants, and also eats, drinks, and gets drunk, the master of that servant will come on a day least expected and at an hour he does not know; he will cut him in pieces and assign him a place with unbelievers.

"The servant who knows what his master wants and did not get ready or act in accordance with his master's desires will be beaten with many lashes. Conversely, whoever did not know and did things worthy of punishment will be beaten with few lashes. From everyone who has been given much, of him will be required much, and from him whom men have entrusted much, they will demand more."

Household Division

LUKE 12:49–59

Jesus continued, saying, "I have come to send fire on the earth—how I wish it were kindled already! I have a baptism to undergo and I am distressed for its completion! Do you think I came to bring peace on earth? I tell you no—I came to bring division. From now on, when you find five members of the same household, there will be division: three against two and two against three; father against son and son against father; daughter against mother and mother against daughter; mother-in-law against daughter-in-law and daughter-in-law against mother-in-law."

Then He turned to the crowd and said, "When you see clouds coming in from the west, you say, 'It is going to rain,' and it does rain. When the wind comes out of the south, you say, 'It is going to be hot,' and it gets hot. Hypocrites! You know how to interpret the appearance of the earth and sky. Why, then, do you not know how to interpret this present time?

"Why do you not judge what is right? Then, when you go with your accuser to the magistrate, make an effort to be reconciled to him while on the way before he drags you in front of the judge, who will turn you over to the officer and he puts you in prison. I tell you that you will not get out of there until you have paid the last cent."

Fruit Bearing

LUKE 13:1–9

About that time some people came up and told Jesus about the Galileans Pilate had killed, mixing their blood with the blood of their sacrifices. Jesus replied to them, saying, "Do you think those murdered Galileans were worse sinners than all the other Galileans because they suffered in this way? I tell you, no! Unless you repent, you will also perish. Do you also think that the eighteen people who were killed when the Tower of Siloam fell on them were guiltier than all the others living in Jerusalem? I tell you, no! Unless you repent, you will also perish."

Then He told them a parable, saying, "A certain man had a fig tree planted in his vineyard and, when he came looking for fruit from it, he did not find any fruit. Then he said to the keeper of his vineyard, 'For three years I have been looking for fruit on this fig tree and have found none. Cut it down. Why should it use up the soil?'

"The gardener replied, 'Sir, leave it alone one more year. I will dig around it and fertilize it. Then, if it bears fruit, fine, but if it does not bear fruit, I will cut it down.'"

Sabbath Healing

LUKE 13:10–17

Jesus was teaching in one of the synagogues on the Sabbath. There was a woman there who, for eighteen years, had a sickness caused by a demon. She was completely bent forward and unable to straighten herself up at all. When Jesus saw her, He called her to Him and said, "Woman, you are released from your sickness." Then He laid His hands on her, and immediately she straightened up, praising God.

The leaders of the synagogue, indignant because Jesus had healed on the Sabbath, said to the crowd, "There are six days in which men ought to work; therefore, come on those days to be healed and not on the Sabbath day."

The Lord replied to him, saying, "You hypocrites! Does not each one of you on the Sabbath untie his ox or his donkey from the stall and lead it out to give it water? Then should not this woman, a daughter of Abraham whom Satan has kept bound for eighteen years, be released from this bond on the Sabbath day?"

When He said this, all His opponents were ashamed, but the people rejoiced because of the wonderful things done by Him.

Narrow Door

LUKE 13:22–35

Jesus went through towns and villages, teaching as He made His way toward Jerusalem.

Someone asked Him, "Lord, are only a few going to be saved?"

Jesus replied, "Strive to enter by the narrow door because many, I tell you, will try to enter and fail. Once the Master of the house gets up and closes the door, you will begin to stand outside and to knock on the door, saying, 'Lord, open up to us.' However, He will answer you, saying, 'I do not know you or from where you come.'

"Then you will say, 'We ate and drank with You and You taught in our streets.'

"He will reply, 'I do not know from where you come. Depart from Me, you workers of iniquity!'

"There will be weeping and gnashing of teeth when you see Jacob and all the prophets in God's kingdom but yourselves cast out. People will come from east, west, north, and south; they will sit down in God's kingdom. Behold, there are some now who are last and they will be first then; there are some now who are first who will be last then."

Just then some Pharisees came up to Him and said, "Go away from here. Herod wants to kill You!"

Jesus said to them, "Tell that fox, 'Behold, I cast out demons and do healings today and tomorrow; on the third day I complete My goal.' Nevertheless, I must continue on My way today, tomorrow, and the next day because no prophet should die outside Jerusalem!

"O Jerusalem, Jerusalem, you who continually kill prophets and stone those sent to you! How often I have yearned to gather your children together, like a hen gathers her chicks under her wings, but you would not allow it! Behold, your house has left you destitute of God's help! I tell you that you will not see Me again until the time comes when you will say, 'Blessed is He Who comes in the name of the Lord!'"

Invitation List

Luke 14:1–14

One time, when Jesus went for a meal with one of the prominent Pharisees on the Sabbath, they were watching Him closely. Right before Him there was a man who had dropsy. Jesus asked the religion experts and Pharisees, "Is it permitted to heal on the Sabbath or not?" They kept silent. Jesus took hold of the man, healed him, and sent him away.

Then Jesus asked them, "Is there anyone here who, if he has a son, donkey, or ox that has fallen into a well, will not immediately pull him out even on the Sabbath?" They were unable to reply to Him on these things.

Jesus told a parable to the guests when He noticed how they chose places of honor for themselves, saying, "When someone invites you to a wedding feast, do not sit down in a place of honor because a more distinguished person than you may have been invited by the host. If this happens, the person who invited both of you will come and say to you, 'Let this man have your seat.' Then, humiliated, you will have to take a less important seat. Therefore, when you are invited, sit in a place of least importance so that when the host comes in, he may say to you, 'Friend, move to a better seat.' As a result, you will be honored in the presence of all the other guests. Everyone who exalts himself will be humbled, and he who humbles himself will be exalted in rank."

Then Jesus said to the host, "When you give a lunch or a dinner, do not invite your friends, brothers, relatives, or rich neighbors; if you do, they may return the favor. Instead, invite the poor, crippled, lame, and blind—you will be blessed because they have no way of repaying you and you will be rewarded at the resurrection of the just."

Invited Guests

LUKE 14:15–24

When one of those who sat at the table with Him heard these things, he said to Jesus, "Blessed is he who shall eat bread in the kingdom of God!"

Jesus replied to him, "A certain man prepared a great dinner and invited many guests. When it was time for dinner, he sent out his servant to the invited guests, saying, 'Come, everything is now ready.'

"However, they all began to make excuses. The first said to him, 'I just bought a piece of land and need to go see it. Please excuse me.'

"Another said, 'I just bought five yoke of oxen and I need to check them out. Please excuse me.'

"Another said, 'I just got married and, therefore, I cannot come to the dinner.'

"The servant went back and reported these things to his master. Then the master of the house said in anger to his servant, 'Go immediately into the streets and alleys of the city; bring in here the poor, crippled, blind, and lame.'

"The servant said, 'Master, I did what you commanded and there is still room.'

"Then the master said, 'Go to the country roads and along the hedges; compel them to come in so my house will be full. I tell you, not one of those originally invited will taste of my dinner.'"

Fund Determination

LUKE 14:25–35

Huge crowds were traveling with Jesus. He turned and said to them, "If anyone comes to Me and does not hate, in comparison with his attitude toward God, his father, mother, wife, children, brothers, and sisters—even his own life—cannot be My disciple. Whoever does not carry his own cross and follow Me cannot be My disciple.

"Which of you, intending to build a tower, does not determine whether he has sufficient funds to complete it? Otherwise, when he has laid the foundation and is unable to finish the building, all who see it will begin to mock him, saying, 'This man began to build and was not able to finish.'

"Or what king goes to wage war against another king without first sitting down and deciding whether he is able with his ten thousand troops to overcome the twenty thousand troops who come against him? If he decides he cannot succeed, when the other king is still a great way off, will he not send an envoy and ask for terms of peace? Likewise, whoever does not forsake all he has cannot be My disciple.

"Salt is good; nevertheless, if the salt loses its saltiness, how can its saltiness be restored again? It is neither fit for the soil nor the manure pile—men throw it away.

"He who has ears to hear, let him comprehend what he hears."

Lost Sheep

MATTHEW 18:10–14
LUKE 15:1–7

Then the tax collectors and notorious sinners drew near to Jesus to listen to Him. The Pharisees and religion experts murmured, saying, "This Man welcomes sinners and eats with them."

Then Jesus told them this parable, saying, "What do you think? Who among you, if he owns a hundred sheep and loses one of them, does not leave the ninety-nine in the wilderness and go after the lost one until he finds it?

"I tell you the truth, if and when he finds it, does he not rejoice more of it than the ninety-nine that did not wander off from the others? When he finds it, he puts it on his shoulders, rejoicing, and when he gets home, he calls his friends and neighbors together and says, 'Rejoice with me because I have found my lost sheep!' I tell you, likewise there will be more joy in heaven over one sinner who repents than over ninety-nine righteous persons who do not need to repent. In the same way, your Father in heaven does not want one of these little ones to perish."

Jesus said to them, "See to it that you do not look down on one of these little ones. I tell you that in heaven their angels are continually in the presence of and see the face of My Father in heaven."

Lost Coin

LUKE 15:8–10

Jesus continued, saying, "What woman who has ten silver coins and loses one will not light a lamp, sweep the house, and diligently search until she finds it? When she finds it she will call her friends and neighbors, saying, 'Rejoice with me because I have found my lost coin.' Likewise, I tell you, there is joy in the presence of the angels of God over one sinner who repents."

Lost Son

LUKE 15:11–32

Then Jesus said, "There was a man who had two sons. The younger one said to his father, 'Father, give me the portion of the property that falls to me.' The father divided his wealth between them.

"Not many days after that, the younger son packed all that he had and journeyed into a country where he wasted his fortune in wild living. When he had spent everything, a severe famine came upon that land

and he began to be in need. He went and joined himself to a citizen of that country who sent him into his fields to feed the hogs. He longed to fill his stomach with the pods the hogs were eating—no one gave him anything better.

"When he came to his senses, he said, 'How many hired servants of my father have enough food to spare and I am dying of hunger! I will get up and go to my father; I will say to him, "Father, I have sinned against heaven and in your sight. I am no longer worthy to be called your son; make me as one of your hired servants."'

"He got up and came to his father. While he was still a long way off, his father saw him and had compassion on him; he ran to his son, embraced him, and kissed him. The son said to him, 'Father, I have sinned against heaven and in your sight. I am no longer worthy to be called your son.' In spite of this, the father said to his servants, 'Quick! Bring the best robe and put it on him. Put a ring on his finger and sandals on his feet. Bring the fattened calf and kill it. Let us eat and be merry because my son was dead and is alive again; he was lost and is found.' They began to celebrate.

"Now the older son was in the field. When he came in and approached the house, he heard the music and dancing. Calling over one of the servants, he asked what was going on at the house. The servant told him, 'Your brother came home and your father has killed the fattened calf because he has him home safe and sound.'

"The older brother was angry, sulked, and refused to go into the house. Therefore, his father came out and pleaded with him, but he would not listen. The son said to his father, 'Look! For many years I have served you and have never disobeyed your commands; yet you never gave me even a young goat so that I might celebrate with my friends. On the other hand, when this son of yours who has squandered your money with prostitutes comes home, you kill for him the fattened calf!'

"His father said, 'Son, you are always with me, and everything that is mine is yours. We had to celebrate because this brother of yours was dead and is alive again; he was lost and he is found!'"

Dishonest Manager

LUKE 16:1–9

Jesus said to His disciples, "There was a certain rich man who had a manager of his estate. Accusations were made to him against this manager of squandering his possessions. So he called him in and said, 'What is this I hear about you? Give an account of your management; you can no longer be my manager.'

"The manager said to himself, 'What shall I do now? My master is taking my job away from me. I am not strong enough to dig and I am ashamed to beg. I know what I will do so that when I lose my job people will welcome me into their houses.'

"So he called each of his master's debtors and asked the first, 'How much do you owe my master?'

"He replied, 'A hundred measures' (about nine hundred gallons) 'of olive oil.'

"The manager said to him, 'Take your bill, sit down quickly, and write fifty' (about four hundred fifty gallons).

"To another he said, 'How much do you owe?'

"He answered, 'A hundred measures' (about nine hundred bushels) 'of wheat.'

"He said to him, 'Take your bill and write down eighty' (seven hundred twenty bushels).

"The master praised the dishonest manager for acting shrewdly; the people of this world are smarter in relation to their own kind than are the sons of light. I say to you, be smart in this way to gain friends for yourself so that, when wealth is gone, they may receive you into eternal dwellings."

Being Trustworthy

LUKE 16:10–18

Jesus continued, saying, "He who can be trusted in a very little thing is also trustworthy in much, and he who is dishonest in a very little thing is also dishonest in much. Consequently, if you cannot be trusted with worldly wealth, who will trust you with true riches? If you have not been trustworthy with that which belongs to another, who will give you property of your own?

"No servant can serve two masters, because he will either hate the one and love the other or he will be devoted to the one and despise the other. You cannot serve both God and money."

The Pharisees, who loved money, heard all these things and scoffed at Jesus; He said to them, "You are the ones who declare yourselves just before men, but God knows your hearts. That which is exalted among men is detestable in the sight of God.

"The law and the prophets were proclaimed until the arrival of John. Since that time, the good news Gospel of the kingdom of God is preached and everyone forces his way into it. However, it is easier for heaven and earth to pass away than for one dot of the law to fail.

"Whoever divorces his wife and marries commits adultery, and whoever marries a divorced woman commits adultery."

Abraham's Side

LUKE 16:19–31

Jesus continued, saying, "There was a certain rich man who habitually dressed in expensive clothes and lived in luxury every day. A certain beggar, named Lazarus, was carelessly laid at his gate. He was covered in sores and desired to be fed with the crumbs that fell from the rich man's table. Moreover, the dogs came and licked his sores.

"It came to pass that the beggar died and was carried by the angels to Abraham's side. The rich man also died and was buried; in hell and in torment, he looked up and saw Abraham far away and Lazarus at his side. He cried out and said, 'Father Abraham, have mercy on me and send Lazarus to dip his finger in water and cool my tongue because I am in agony in this flame!'

"However, Abraham said, 'Son, remember that in your lifetime you received the good things, while Lazarus received the bad things, but now he is comforted here and you are in torment. Beside all this, there is a great chasm between us so that no one can go from us to you, nor can anyone cross over from you to us.'

"The rich man answered, 'Then I beg you, father, to send Lazarus to my father's house, where I have five brothers, so he can testify and warn them so they do not also come into this place of torment.'

"Abraham said to him, 'They have Moses and the prophets; let them listen to them.'

"He replied, 'No, father Abraham; but if someone came back to them from the dead, they will repent.'

"Abraham said to him, 'If they do not listen to Moses and the prophets, neither will they be persuaded if someone rises from the dead.'"

Two Agree

MATTHEW 18:15–20

Jesus continued, saying, "If your brother sins against you, go and tell him his fault between the two of you privately. If he listens, you have won back your brother. Nevertheless, if he does not listen to you, take one or two others with you so that every word may be confirmed by two or three witnesses. If he refuses to listen to them, tell it to the church. If he refuses to listen to the church, treat him as you would a pagan or a tax collector.

"I tell you the truth, a yes on earth is yes in heaven and a no on earth is no in heaven.

"Again I tell you, if two of you on earth agree about anything you ask, it shall be done for you by My Father in heaven. Where two or three are gathered in My name, I am in their midst."

Increase Faith

LUKE 17:1–10

Jesus said to His disciples, "It is inevitable that temptations that cause people to sin are sure to come, but woe to him through whom they come! It would be better for him if a millstone was hung around his neck and he was thrown into the sea than for him to cause one of these little ones to sin.

"Be on your guard for each other. If your brother sins, rebuke him; if he repents, forgive him. Even if he sins against you seven times a day and comes to you each time, saying, 'I repent,' forgive him."

The apostles said to the Lord, "Increase our faith."

The Lord answered, "If you had faith as small as a mustard seed, you could say to this mulberry tree, 'Be uprooted and planted in the sea,' and it would obey you.

"Would any of you who had a servant plowing or tending sheep say to him when he came in from the field, 'Come immediately and sit down to eat'? No, he would instead tell him, 'Prepare my meal, change your clothes, and serve me while I eat and drink; afterward you will eat and drink.' Does he thank the servant for doing what is expected of him? It is the same with you. When you have done everything you are supposed to do, you should say, 'We are unworthy servants; we have merely done our duty.'"

Forgiving Others

MATTHEW 18:21–35

Then Peter came to Jesus and asked, "How many times shall my brother sin against me and I forgive him? Shall I forgive him up to seven times?"

Jesus replied, "I tell you, not up to seven times but seventy times seven.

"Therefore, the kingdom of heaven is like a king who desired to settle accounts with his servants. When he began, one servant was brought to him who owed him ten thousand talents" (ten million dollars). "Since he could not pay, his master ordered him to be sold with his wife, children, and all his possessions to repay the debt.

"The servant fell on his knees and begged, 'Have patience with me and I will repay you everything.' Then the servant's master was moved with compassion—he canceled the debt and released him.

"In spite of this, the same servant went out and found one of his fellow servants who owed him a hundred denarii" (twenty dollars). "He seized him by the throat and demanded, 'Pay me what you owe me!'

"The fellow servant fell on his knees and begged, 'Have patience with me and I will repay you.'

"Nevertheless, he would not do it. He had him arrested and put in jail until he could pay the debt. When his fellow servants saw what happened, they were greatly distressed; they came and told what had taken place to the king.

"The king summoned the man and said, 'You wicked servant! I canceled your entire debt because you begged me. Should you not also have mercy on your fellow servant just as I had mercy on you?' The king was angry and turned him over to the jailer to be tortured until he could repay the debt.

"This is what My heavenly Father is going to do to every one of you if you do not forgive your brother, from your heart, his trespasses."

Ten Lepers

LUKE 17:11–19

It came to pass, as Jesus was on His way to Jerusalem, He crossed the border between Samaria and Galilee. As He entered a town, He was met by ten men who had leprosy. They kept their distance but raised their voices, saying, "Jesus, Master, have mercy on us!"

When He saw them, He said to them, "Go, show yourselves to the priests." As they went they were made clean.

One of them, when he saw that he was healed, came back and praised God in a loud voice. He threw himself prostrate at Jesus' feet, giving Him thanks. He was a Samaritan.

Then Jesus asked, "Were not ten made clean? Where are the other nine? Can none be found to come back and give glory to God except this outsider?" Then He said to him, "Get up and go on your way. Your faith has made you well."

Jesus' Arrival

Luke 17:20–37

When Jesus was asked by the Pharisees when the kingdom of God would come, He replied, "The kingdom of God does not come with observable signs, nor will people say, 'Here it is,' or 'There it is,' because the kingdom of God is within you."

Then He said to His disciples, "The time is coming when you will desire to see one of the days of the Son of Man and you will not see it. They will say to you, 'Look over there!' or 'Look here!' Do not go after or follow them because, just like the lightning that flashes and lights up the sky, so will the Son of Man be in His day. However, first He must suffer many things and be rejected by this generation.

"Just as it was in Noah's day, so it will be in the days of the Son of Man. People ate, drank, married, and were given in marriage up to the day Noah entered the ark. Then the flood came and destroyed all of them.

"It was the same in the days of Lot—the people were eating, drinking, buying, selling, planting, and building, but on the day Lot left Sodom, it rained fire and brimstone from heaven and destroyed all of them.

"That is the way it will be on the day the Son of Man is revealed to you. On that day, no one who is on the roof of his house, with his belongings inside, should come down to get them. Likewise, no one in the field should go back for anything. Remember Lot's wife! Whoever tries to save his life will lose it and whoever loses his life will save it. I tell you, on that night there will be two men in one bed; one will be taken and the other left. Two women will be grinding grain together; one will be taken and the other left."

Then they asked Him, "Where, Lord?"

Jesus replied, "Wherever the dead body is, there the vultures will gather together."

Never Quit

LUKE 18:1–8

Jesus told His disciples a parable to show them they should always pray and never quit. He said, "There was a judge in a certain city who did not fear God and cared nothing for people. There was a widow in that city who kept coming to him, saying, 'Give me protection against my adversary.'

"For a while he was unwilling, but afterward he said to himself, 'Even though I do not fear God and care nothing for people, yet because this widow keeps bothering me, I will give her protection so that she does not wear me out by her continually coming to me.'"

Then the Lord said, "Listen what that unjust judge says. Will not our just God protect His elect who cry out to Him day and night? Will He keep putting them off? I tell you, He will quickly protect them. However, how much of that kind of persistent faith will the Son of Man find on the earth when He returns?"

Be Humble

LUKE 18:9–14

Jesus told a parable to some people who trusted in themselves that they were righteous and looked down on others, saying, "Two men went up to the temple to pray; one was a Pharisee and the other a tax collector.

The Pharisee stood and prayed to himself, saying, 'God, I thank You that I am not like other people—robbers, swindlers, adulterers, or even like this tax collector. I fast twice a week and tithe on all my income.'

"Meanwhile, the tax collector stood at a distance and would not even lift up his eyes to heaven; he kept beating his chest, saying, 'God, be merciful to me, a sinner.'"

Jesus commented, "I tell you, this tax collector, rather than the other, went home justified before God. Everyone who exalts himself will be humbled, but those who humble themselves will be exalted before God."

Chapter 7

JESUS' LAST MINISTRY

Lawful Divorce

MATTHEW 19:1–12
MARK 10:1–12

When Jesus had finished saying these things, He left Galilee and came to the region of Judea on the other side of the Jordan River. Again, crowds gathered around Him and followed Him there. As was His custom, He taught them and healed them.

Some Pharisees also came to Him and tested Him, saying, "Is it lawful for a man to divorce his wife for any reason?"

Jesus answered, "What did Moses command you?"

They said, "Moses permitted a man to write a certificate of divorce and send her away."

Jesus said, "It was because of the hardness of your hearts that Moses wrote you this law. Have you not read that the Creator, in the beginning, made them male and female, saying, 'For this reason a man leaves his father and mother to be firmly united to his wife—the two become one flesh'? They become one flesh and are no longer two individuals. Hence, what God has joined together, let not man separate."

They said to Him, "Why then did Moses command that a man give his wife a certificate of divorce and send her away?"

Jesus said, "It was because of the hardness of your hearts that Moses permitted you to divorce your wives. Nevertheless, from the beginning it was not this way. I say to you, whoever divorces his wife, except for marital unfaithfulness, and marries another woman commits adultery; whoever marries a divorced woman commits adultery."

When they were in the house again, the disciples questioned Jesus about this subject. He said to them, "Whoever divorces his wife and marries another commits adultery against her, and a woman who divorces her husband and marries someone else commits adultery."

Jesus' disciples said to Him, "If the relationship of a man with his wife is like that, it is better not to marry."

Jesus replied, "Not all men can accept this saying; it is only for those to whom has been given the capacity to receive it. There are eunuchs who were born incapable of marriage. There are men who were made eunuchs by men. There are eunuchs who made themselves that way—renouncing marriage—for the sake of the kingdom of heaven. He who is able to accept this should accept it."

Children Blessed

Matthew 19:13–15
Mark 10:13–16
Luke 18:15–17

One day the people brought children and babies so that He might touch them—that He would lay hands on them—and pray for them. When the disciples saw it, they rebuked those who brought them. However, when Jesus saw this, He called them—parents and children—to Him because He was very displeased with His disciples. He said, "Allow the children to come to Me; do not hinder them from coming to Me, because to such belongs the kingdom of God. I tell you the truth, whoever does not receive the kingdom of God like a little child will never enter it." Then He took the children in His arms, placed His hands on them, and blessed them. Then He departed from there.

Rich Man

MATTHEW 19:16–30
MARK 10:17–31
LUKE 18:18–30

Behold, as Jesus started out on a journey, a man, a certain ruler, ran up and knelt before Him, asking, "Good Teacher, what good thing must I do to inherit eternal life?"

Jesus replied, "Why do you call Me good? Why do you question Me about what is good? No one is good, only God—He is the One Who is good. If you want to enter the life of God, continually obey the commandments."

The man asked, "Which ones?"

Jesus said, "You know the commandments: Do not commit adultery; do not murder; do not steal; do not give false witness; do not defraud; honor your father and mother; love your neighbor as you do yourself."

The young man said to Him, "Teacher, I have observed all these things since I was a youth. What do I still lack?"

When Jesus heard that, He looked at him and loved him. Then He said to him, "One thing you lack. If you wish to be perfect, go, sell your possessions, and give to the poor—you will have treasure in heaven. Then come follow Me."

At these words the man sadly went away because he was wealthy with many possessions.

When Jesus saw his deep sadness, He looked at His disciples and said, "I tell you the truth, it is difficult for a rich man to enter the kingdom of heaven!" The disciples were bewildered at His words. Jesus continued, saying, "Children, how hard it is for those who trust in riches to enter the kingdom of God. Again I tell you, it is easier for a camel to go through a needle's eye than for a rich man to enter the kingdom of God."

When the disciples heard this, they were even more astonished and said to each other and to Jesus, "Who can be saved then?"

Jesus looked at them and said, "With men this is impossible but not with God—with God all things are possible."

Then Peter said to Him, "Behold, we have left everything we owned to follow You! What then will there be for us?"

Jesus said to them, "To you who have followed Me, I tell you the truth, at the regeneration of all things when the Son of Man will sit on the throne of His glory, you will also sit on twelve thrones and judge the twelve tribes of Israel. No one who has left houses, brothers, sisters, father, mother, wife, children, or land for My name's sake, for the Gospel and the kingdom of God will fail to receive a hundred times as much—houses, brothers, sisters, mother, children, and land (and with them, persecutions)—in this present age and, in the age to come, eternal life. Many who are now first will be last then, and many who are now last will be first then."

Workers' Pay

MATTHEW 20:1–16

Jesus continued, saying, "The kingdom of heaven is like an estate owner who went out early in the morning to hire laborers for his vineyard. When they agreed on a wage of a denarius for the day, he sent them into his vineyard.

"The owner went out about the third hour" (nine o'clock in the morning) "and saw some other men standing idle in the marketplace. He said to them, 'You also go into my vineyard and I will pay you whatever is right.' So they went to work in his vineyard.

"He did the same thing at the sixth hour" (noon) "and the ninth hour" (three o'clock in the afternoon). "About the eleventh hour" (five o'clock in the afternoon), "he went out and found others standing around. He said to them, 'Why have you been standing here idle all day?'

"They answered, 'Because no one hired us.'

"He said to them, 'You, too, go to work in my vineyard.'"

"When evening came, the owner of the vineyard said to his foreman, 'Call the laborers and pay them their wages. Begin with the last ones hired and go on to the first.'"

"Those who had been hired at the eleventh hour" (five o'clock in the afternoon) "received one denarius each. When those who were hired first came, they thought they would receive more. However, each of them received one denarius. When they received it, they murmured against the owner of the estate, saying, 'These men who were hired last only worked one hour and you have made them equal to us who have borne the burden of work and the scorching heat of the day.'"

"The owner replied to one of them, saying, 'I am doing you no wrong. Did you not agree with me to work for a denarius? Take your pay and go home. I wish to give the man hired last the same as I gave you. Do I not have the right to do this? Is your eye envious because I am generous?'"

"I say again, those who now are last will be first then, and those who now are first will be last then."

Jesus' Sheep

JOHN 10:22–42

At that time, the Feast of Dedication was taking place in Jerusalem. It was winter and Jesus was walking in the temple area in Solomon's Porch. The Jews, surrounding Him, said, "How long are You going to keep us in doubt? If You are the Christ, tell us plainly."

Jesus answered them, saying, "I told you but you do not believe. The miracles that I do in My Father's name bear witness of Me. You do not believe because you are not My sheep. My sheep listen to My voice; I know them and they follow Me. I give them eternal life and they shall never perish—no one can snatch them out of My hand. My Father Who gave them to Me is greater than all. No one is able to snatch them out of My Father's hand. I and the Father are One."

Again the Jews picked up stones to stone Him. Jesus said, "I have shown you many miracles from My Father. For which of these do you stone Me?"

The Jews replied, "We are not going to stone You for anything good You did but for blasphemy, because You, being a man, make Yourself out to be God."

Jesus answered, "Is it not written in your law, 'I have said you are gods'? If He called them gods to whom the word of God came, and Scripture cannot be broken, why do you say to Me, the One Whom the Father sanctified and sent into the world, 'You are blaspheming,' because I said, 'I am the Son of God'? If I do not perform the works of My Father, do not believe Me. However, if I do them, even though you do not believe Me, believe the miracles so that you may know and clearly understand that the Father is in Me and I am in the Father." Again they sought to arrest Him, but He escaped from their hands.

Then Jesus went back across the Jordan River to the place where John first baptized and stayed there. Many people came to Him and were saying, "John performed no miracles, but everything he said about this Man was true." Many believed in Jesus in that place.

Lazarus' Death

JOHN 11:1–44

A certain man was sick, Lazarus of Bethany, the town of Mary and her sister Martha. This Mary was the one who anointed the Lord with perfume and wiped His feet with her hair. It was her brother Lazarus who was sick. So the sisters sent word to Jesus, "Lord, the one You love is sick."

When Jesus received the message, He said, "This sickness will not end in death. On the contrary, it is for the glory of God so that the Son of God may be glorified by it." Jesus loved Martha, her sister, and Lazarus. Yet, when He heard he was sick, He stayed where He was two days longer.

Then Jesus said to His disciples, "Let us go back to Judea again."

Jesus' disciples said to Him, "Rabbi, the Jews recently were trying to stone You. Are You going back there again?"

Jesus answered, "Are there not twelve hours of daylight in the day? Anyone who walks in daylight does not stumble because he sees by this world's light. However, anyone who walks about in the night, he does stumble because the light is not in him."

After He said these things, He went on to say, "Our friend Lazarus has fallen asleep. I am going there to wake him up."

His disciples said, "Lord, if he is sleeping, he will recover." However, Jesus was talking about his death, while His disciples thought He was talking about natural sleep.

Then Jesus told them plainly, "Lazarus is dead. I am glad for your sakes that I was not there. It will help you believe in Me. Nevertheless, let us go to him."

Then Thomas, called Didymus (the Twin), said to his fellow disciples, "Let us also go that we may die with Him."

When Jesus arrived, He found Lazarus already dead and that he had been in the tomb four days. Bethany was near Jerusalem, about fifteen furlongs (two miles) away. Many of the Jews were visiting Martha and Mary to comfort them concerning their brother. When Martha heard that Jesus was coming, she went to meet Him, but Mary remained sitting in the house.

Then Martha said to Jesus, "Master, if You had been here, my brother would not have died. Even now, I know that whatever You ask of God, He will give You."

Jesus said to her, "Your brother shall rise again."

Martha replied, "I know that he will rise again in the resurrection at the last day."

Jesus said to her, "I am the Resurrection and the Life. The one who believes in Me, even though he dies, yet shall he live. Everyone who lives believing in Me shall never die at all. Do you believe this?"

She said to Him, "Yes, Lord, I believe that You are the Christ, the Son of God, Who was to come into the world."

After saying this, she went back and called her sister Mary and privately whispered to her, "The Teacher is here and is asking for you." As soon as she heard this, she got up quickly and went to Him. Jesus had not yet entered the town but was still at the place where Martha had met Him. Then the Jews who were with her in the house comforting her saw how quickly she got up and went out, followed her saying, "She is going to the tomb to weep there."

Mary came to where Jesus was waiting and saw Him; she fell at His feet, saying, "Lord, if You had been here, my brother would not have died."

When Jesus saw her weeping, and the Jews with her were also weeping, He was deeply moved in spirit and He was troubled at that time. He said, "Where have you laid him?"

They said to Him, "Lord, come and see."

Jesus wept.

The Jews said, "See how deeply He loved him."

Some of them said, "Could not this Man, Who opened the eyes of the blind man, have kept this man from dying?"

Then Jesus, deeply moved again, came to the tomb. It was a cave with a stone laid against it. Jesus said, "Remove the stone."

Martha, the sister of the dead man, said, "Lord, by this time there will be a stench because he has been dead four days!"

Jesus said to her, "Did I not tell you that if you believed in Me you would see the glory of God?"

When they had removed the stone, Jesus raised His eyes toward heaven and prayed, "Father, I thank You that You have heard Me. I know that You always do listen to Me, but on account of the people standing here, I have spoken so that they might believe that You sent Me."

After Jesus said this, He shouted with a loud voice, "Lazarus, come out!" He who had died came out, his hands and feet wrapped in linen cloth strips and with a burial cloth around his face.

Jesus told them, "Unwrap him and let him go."

Miracle Man

JOHN 11:45–57

When many of the Jews who had come to Mary saw what Jesus had done, they believed on Him. However, some of them went to the Pharisees and told them what Jesus had done in Bethany. Then the chief priests and Pharisees called a meeting of the Sanhedrin.

They said, "What are we going to do now? This Man is performing many miracles. If we let Him go on like this, everyone will believe in Him and the Romans will come and take away both our holy place and our nation."

Then one of them—Caiaphas, who was high priest that year—spoke up: "You know nothing at all. You do not understand that it is better for us that one Man should die for the people than that the entire nation should perish."

He did not say this on his own accord, but since he was high priest that year, he unwittingly prophesied that Jesus was going to die for the nation; not only for the nation but also for the purpose of gathering together the children of God, who had been scattered, and uniting them. Then from that day on they plotted to put Him to death.

Consequently, Jesus no longer appeared publicly among the Jews; He left there and went to the region near the desert, to the town of Ephraim, where He stayed with His disciples.

The Jewish Feast of Passover was at hand, and many went from the country to Jerusalem before the Passover to purify themselves. They kept looking for Jesus and were saying to each other as they stood in the temple area, "What do you think? Will He come to the Feast of Passover at all?" Now the chief priests and Pharisees had given orders that if anyone knew where He was, he should report it to them so that they could arrest Him.

Be Servants

MATTHEW 20:17–28
MARK 10:32–45
LUKE 18:31–34

When they were on their way to Jerusalem, Jesus was walking in front of His disciples; they were bewildered, and those who still followed were fearful. Jesus took the twelve disciples aside and said to them, "We are going up to Jerusalem. Everything written about the Son of Man by the prophets will take place. The Son of Man will be betrayed to the religious leaders and religion experts. They will sentence Him to death. They will turn Him over to the Gentiles—Romans—who will mock Him, spit on Him, flog Him, and kill Him by crucifixion. On the third day He will be raised up alive." The disciples did not understand these things—the meaning was hidden from them. They did not know what He was talking about.

Then the mother of the Zebedee sons, James and John, came with them, knelt before Jesus, and asked a favor of Him, saying, "We want You to do for us whatever we ask You."

Jesus asked, "What do you want Me to do for you?"

She said, "Grant that my two sons may sit, one at Your right hand and one at Your left hand, in Your kingdom."

Jesus said, "You do not realize what you are asking from Me." Then He said to James and John, "Are you able to drink the cup that I am about to drink and be baptized with the baptism I am about to be afflicted with soon?"

They said, "We are able."

Jesus said to them, "You will indeed drink from My cup and you will be baptized with the baptism I am afflicted with soon, but to sit at My right hand and at My left hand are not Mine to give to you. These places belong to those for whom it has been prepared by My Father."

When the other ten disciples heard about this, they were indignant with James and John. So Jesus got them together and said, "You know that the rulers of the Gentiles lord it over them, and their great men exercise authority over them. However, it will not be so among you. Whoever wants to be great among you must be your servant, just as the Son of Man came not to be served but to serve and to give His life as a ransom for many."

Sight Restored

MATTHEW 20:29–34
MARK 10:46–52
LUKE 18:35–43

Jesus and His disciples came to the old town Jericho. As they were leaving and were at the outskirts of town, with a large crowd of people behind them, they came upon two blind men sitting by the road begging for handouts. One of the blind men was named Bartimaeus, son of Timaeus. When they heard the crowd going by, he asked what was going on. They told him, "Jesus of Nazareth is going by." Bartimaeus shouted, "Jesus, Son of David! Lord, have mercy on us!" The crowd told them to be quiet, but they shouted louder, "Jesus, Son of David! Lord, have mercy on us!"

Jesus stopped and ordered them to be brought to Him, saying, "Call him over." They called them, saying, "Take courage! Get up! He is calling you!" Throwing off his cloak, he jumped to his feet and came to Jesus. When they came near, Jesus asked, "What do you want Me to do for you?"

The blind man said, "Rabbi, Lord, we want to see again."

Jesus, moved with compassion, touched their eyes and said, "Receive your sight. Be on your way. Your faith has healed you." Immediately they received their sight and followed Him down the road, praising God. All the people, when they saw this, gave praise to God.

Zacchaeus Visited

LUKE 19:1–10

Then Jesus entered and walked through the new town of Jericho. There was a man there named Zacchaeus. He was the chief tax collector and he was very rich. He was trying to see who Jesus was, but he was unable on account of the crowd because he was a short man. So he ran ahead and climbed up a sycamore tree in order to see Him, since Jesus was about to pass that way.

When Jesus came to the place, He looked up and said to him, "Zacchaeus, hurry and come down. Today I will be a guest in your house." Zacchaeus quickly came down and welcomed Him gladly.

When the people saw this, they grumbled, saying, "He has gone to be the guest of a man who is a sinner."

Zacchaeus stood up and said to the Lord, "Behold, Lord, Master, I give away half my possessions to the poor and, if I have cheated anyone, I will give back four times as much."

Jesus said to him, "Today salvation has come to this house because Zacchaeus, too, is a son of Abraham. The Son of Man came to seek and save that which was lost."

Well Done

LUKE 19:11–27

While they were listening to these things, Jesus proceeded to tell them a parable because He was near Jerusalem and the people's expectation was building that God's kingdom would appear immediately. He, therefore, said, "A certain nobleman went to a distant country to obtain for himself a kingdom and then return. He called ten of his servants, gave them ten minas" (three months' wages), "and said, 'Put this money to work until I come back.'

"However, his subjects detested him and sent a delegation after him, saying, 'We do not want this man to rule us.'

"It came to pass that when he returned, after having received the kingdom, he ordered the servants to whom he had given the money to be called to him so that he might know what they had gained with the money.

"The first said, 'Lord, your mina has made ten additional minas.'

"He said, 'Well done, my good servant! Because you have been trustworthy in a very little, you shall have authority over ten cities.'

"The second said, 'Lord, your mina has made five additional minas.'

"He said likewise, 'You shall have authority over five cities.'

"The next servant said, 'Lord, here is your mina, which I have kept put away in a napkin. I was afraid of you because you are a hard man. You pick up what you did not lay down and you reap what you did not sow.'

"Then he replied to the servant, 'I will judge you by your own words, you wicked servant. You knew I was a hard man, picking up what I did not lay down and reaping what I did not sow. Why, then, did you not put my money in a bank so that when I returned, I could have collected it with interest?'

"Then he said to those standing there, 'Take the mina from him and give it to the servant who has ten minas.'

"They said, 'Lord, he has ten minas already!'

"He replied, 'I tell you that to everyone who has, more will be given, and from him who does not have, even what he has will be taken away from him. However, these enemies of mine who did not want me to reign over them, bring them here and kill them in my presence!'"

Feet Anointed

JOHN 12:1–11

Six days before Passover, Jesus came to Bethany where Lazarus lived, whom He raised from the dead. They made Him dinner and Martha served, but Lazarus was one of those reclining at the table with Him.

Mary took a pound (about a pint) of pure liquid nard—a rare and expensive perfume—and anointed Jesus' feet. Then she wiped His feet with her hair. The house was filled with the fragrance of the perfume.

Then one of His disciples, Judas Iscariot, Simon's son, who would later betray Him, said, "Why was the perfume not sold for three hundred denarii" (a year's wages) "and given to the poor?" He did not say this because he cared for the poor but because he was a thief. Since he kept the money bag for the Twelve, he pilfered for himself the money put into it.

Then Jesus said, "Let her alone. She saved the perfume so that she might have it for My burial. You always have the poor with you, but you do not always have Me."

Meanwhile, a great number of Jews learned that He was at Bethany and came there, not only because of Jesus but also so they might see Lazarus, whom He had raised from the dead. So the chief priests planned to also kill Lazarus because so many of the Jews were going over to Jesus and believing in Him.

Chapter 8

JESUS' LAST WEEK

Triumphal Entry

MATTHEW 21:1–11
MARK 11:1–11
LUKE 19:28–44
JOHN 12:12–19

After saying these things, Jesus went on ahead of them, ascending to Jerusalem. The next day the great crowd that had come to the Feast of Passover heard that Jesus was coming to Jerusalem. They took palm tree branches and went out to meet Him, shouting, "Hosanna! Blessed is He Who comes in the name of the Lord! Blessed is the King of Israel!"

When they neared Jerusalem and arrived at Bethphage and Bethany at the hill called the Mount of Olives, Jesus sent ahead two of His disciples, saying to them, "Go into the town opposite you. As soon as you enter, you will find a donkey tied there with her colt—one that has never been ridden by anyone. Untie them and bring them to Me. If anyone asks, 'Why are you doing this?' say, 'The Lord needs them and will return them right away!' He will send them with you."

All this was done to fulfill what was spoken by the prophet, saying as written in Scripture, "Fear not, daughter of Zion; behold, your King comes to you, meek and riding a donkey colt, the foal of a beast of burden." The disciples did not understand the meaning of these things at first, but when Jesus was glorified, they remembered that these things were written and they had done these things to Him.

The two disciples went ahead and found them just as He had told them, and they did exactly what Jesus told them. They found the donkey and colt tied by a door and untied them. As they did so, some people standing there—the owners—asked them, "Why are you untying that colt?" The disciples replied as Jesus had instructed them, saying, "The Lord needs it." They brought the donkey and colt to Jesus. Then they laid and threw their garments on them. Jesus sat on the clothing. Many people spread their garments on the road. Others cut branches from the trees and spread them on the road. Crowds that went ahead of Him and the crowds that followed after Him—the entire crowd of disciples—when Jesus approached the city at the descent of the Mount of Olives, began to rejoice and praise God with a loud voice for all the mighty miracles they had seen, shouting,

> Hosanna to the Son of David!
> Blessed is He, the King, Who comes in the name of the Lord!
> Blessed be the kingdom of our father David that comes in the name
>   of the Lord!
> Peace in heaven and glory in the highest!
> Hosanna in the highest heaven!

The crowd that had been with Him when He called Lazarus from the tomb, raising him from the dead, were bearing witness of Him. For this reason the people went to meet Jesus—they heard He had performed this miracle. The Pharisees said to each other, "Your efforts are futile. The whole world is gone after Him."

Some Pharisees from the crowd said to Him, "Teacher, rebuke Your disciples!"

Jesus answered, "I tell you, if they kept silent, the stones would immediately cry out!"

When the city came into view, He wept over it and said, "If you, even you, knew on this day the thing that would bring you peace! However, now they are hidden from your eyes. A time is coming when your enemies will build an embankment against you, surround you, and hem you in on every side. They will level you to the ground and your children within you. They will not leave in you one stone upon another because you did not recognize the time of your visitation from God."

When Jesus entered Jerusalem, and then the temple, He looked around at everything. The entire city was stirred—the people were asking, "Who is this?" The crowd replied, "This is Jesus the Prophet from Nazareth in Galilee." Since it was already late, He departed for Bethany with the Twelve.

Tables Overturned

MATTHEW 21:12–17
MARK 11:12–19
LUKE 19:45–48

As they left Bethany the next day, Jesus was hungry. He saw in the distance a fig tree covered with leaves. He went to see if He could find any fruit on it, but when He came to it, He found nothing but leaves—it was not the season for figs. Jesus said to the tree, "No one shall ever eat fruit from you again." His disciples heard Him say it.

When they arrived at Jerusalem, Jesus went into the temple. He immediately began driving out everyone who bought and sold in the temple area. He turned over the tables of the moneychangers and the seats of those who sold doves and pigeons. He would not permit anyone to carry any merchandise through the temple. He taught them, saying,

"It is written in Scripture, 'My house shall be called a house of prayer for all nations. However, you have made it a den of thieves.'"

He taught each day in the temple. The blind and lame came to Him there and He healed them. When the chief priests and religion experts heard what was going on, along with the leaders of the people, and saw the wonderful things He was doing, they sought for a way to kill Him because they feared Him; they could not find any way to do it because the people hung on His words—they were astonished at His teaching. When the chief priests and religion experts heard the children in the temple area shouting, "Hosanna to the Son of David," they were displeased and indignant. They said to Him, "Do You hear what they are saying about You?" Jesus replied, "Yes, have you never read, 'From the mouths of children and infants You have perfected praise'?"

Jesus left them, and when evening came, He and His disciples went out of the city to Bethany, where they spent the night.

Withered Tree

MATTHEW 21:18–22
MARK 11:20–26

In the morning, as they passed by, they saw that the fig tree was completely withered from the roots. Peter remembered what happened the previous day: Early in the morning, as Jesus was returning to the city, He was hungry; seeing a single fig tree by the road, He came to it but found nothing but fig leaves; He said to it, "Never again shall fruit grow on you"; the fig tree withered immediately. When the disciples saw it, they marveled and said to Him, "Master, look, the fig tree You cursed has withered away so quickly!"

Jesus answered and said to them, "I tell you the truth, whoever has faith and does not doubt, they will not only do what has been done to the fig tree, but even if they say to this mountain, 'Remove yourself and be cast into the sea,' it will happen—it will be done for them. All things you ask for, believing in prayer, you will have it done for you.

Therefore, I say to you, whatever you ask for in prayer, believe that it is granted to you and you shall have it. When you stand praying, if you have anything against anyone, forgive him so that your Father Who is in heaven may forgive you of your sins."

What Authority?

MATTHEW 21:23–27
MARK 11:27–33
LUKE 20:1–8

One day they came to Jerusalem again. Jesus was teaching the people as He walked in the temple, and preaching the Gospel. The chief priests and religion experts came to Him with the elders of the people, saying to Him, "Tell us by what authority are You doing these things and who gave You this authority?"

Jesus answered and said to them, "First I will ask you a question, and if you answer My question, then I will tell you by what authority I do these things. The baptism of John, where did it come from? Was it from heaven or from men? Answer Me!"

They reasoned with themselves, saying, "If we say, 'from heaven,' He will ask us why we did not believe John. If we say, 'from men,' we fear the people will stone us because they are convinced John was a prophet." So they replied, "We do not know."

Jesus said to them, "Neither will I tell you by what authority I am doing these things."

Two Sons

MATTHEW 21:28–32

Then Jesus said, "What do you think? A man had two sons. He came to the first and said, 'Son, go work today in my vineyard.'

"The son answered, 'I will not,' but afterward changed his mind and went to work.

153

"The man came to the second son and said the same thing. He answered, 'I will go, sir,' but he did not go to work.

"Which of the two sons did the father's will?"

They said to Him, "The first."

Jesus said to them, "I tell you the truth, tax collectors and prostitutes will get into the kingdom of God before you. John came to you to show you the way of righteousness and you did not believe him, but the tax collectors and prostitutes did believe him. Even after you saw, you did not repent and believe him."

New Tenants

MATTHEW 21:33–46
MARK 12:1–12
LUKE 20:9–19

Jesus began to speak to the people, saying, "Listen to another parable. There was a landowner who planted a vineyard. He put a wall around it, dug a winepress in it, and built a watchtower. Then he rented it out to tenants and went off on a journey for a long time. When it was time to harvest the grapes, he sent his servants to the tenants to collect some of the fruit of the vineyard.

"However, the tenants grabbed the first servant, beat him, and sent him away empty-handed. Then he sent another servant to them. They stoned him, wounded him in the head, treated him shamefully, and sent him away empty-handed. He sent a third servant; they wounded him and threw him out of the vineyard. The landowner sent another and they killed him. Then he sent another group of servants, more than the first time, and the tenants treated them the same way—some they beat and they killed others. Then the landowner of the vineyard said, 'What shall I do? I will send my beloved son; perhaps they will respect him.' So last of all he sent his son to them, saying, 'They will respect my son.'

"Nevertheless, when the tenants saw the son, they said to each other, 'This is the heir. Let us kill him so that the inheritance will be ours.' So they took him, killed him, and threw him out of the vineyard.

"Now, when the owner of the vineyard comes home, what will he do to the tenants?"

They said to Him, "He will kill those wicked tenants and give the vineyard to other tenants who will give him his share of the fruit at harvest time."

When they heard this, they said, "God forbid!" Jesus said to them, "Have you never read the Scripture? What is the meaning of what is written?

That Stone which the builders rejected
has become the Cornerstone.
This is the Lord's doing and it is marvelous in our eyes.

"As a result, I tell to you that the kingdom of God will be taken away from you and given to people who will produce fruit. Whoever falls on this Stone will be broken in pieces, but whoever the Stone falls on will be ground to powder."

When the religion experts, chief priests, and Pharisees heard Jesus' parable, they understood He was talking about them. Although they desired to arrest Him, they feared the crowd because they regarded Him as a prophet. For that reason, they left Him and went away.

Wedding Banquet

MATTHEW 22:1–14

Jesus again spoke to them in parables, saying, "The kingdom of heaven is like a king who gave a wedding banquet for his son. He sent his servants to summon those who were invited to the wedding, but they refused to come to the banquet.

"He sent other servants, saying, 'Tell those who are invited, "Behold, I have prepared my banquet—my oxen and fattened cattle have been butchered and everything is ready. Come to the wedding banquet."'

"Nevertheless, they paid no attention and went their way—one to his farm and another to his business. The others seized his servants, mistreated them, and then killed them. When the king heard this, he was enraged; he sent his armies to kill those murderers and burn their city.

"Then he said to his servants, 'The wedding is ready, but the invited guests were not worthy. Therefore, go to the streets and invite anyone you find to the banquet.' Those servants went to the streets and gathered all they could find, both bad and good; the wedding hall was filled with guests.

"When the king came to see the guests, he saw a man there who was not dressed in wedding clothes. He said to him, 'Friend, how did you come in here without wedding clothes?' The man was speechless.

"Then the king told his servants, 'Tie him hand and foot. Take him away and cast him into the outer darkness where there will be weeping and gnashing of teeth.'

"Many are invited but few are chosen."

Pharisee Trap

MATTHEW 22:15–22
MARK 12:13–17
LUKE 20:20–26

Then the Pharisees plotted together how they might trap Him with His words. They watched Him and sent spies—Pharisees and Herodians who pretended to be honest—to Jesus to trap Him in a statement so they could turn Him over to the control and authority of the governor. They came to Him and questioned Him, saying, "Teacher, we know You are truthful, teach what is right, teach the way of God truthfully, are not biased for anyone, and pay no attention to the position of anyone.

Therefore, tell us Your opinion. Is it lawful to pay taxes to Caesar or not?"

However, Jesus perceived their evil intent and said, "You hypocrites, why are you trying to trap Me? Bring Me a denarius coin used to pay taxes so I may look at it." They brought Him the coin. Then He asked them, "Whose image and name are on it?"

They said, "Caesar's."

Then He said to them, "Give to Caesar the things that are Caesar's and to God the things that are God's."

They were unable to trap Him for what He said before the people. They were amazed at Him, became silent, and went away.

Resurrection Marriage

MATTHEW 22:23–33
MARK 12:18–27
LUKE 20:27–40

The same day, some Sadducees, who say there is no resurrection, came to Jesus and asked Him a question, saying, "Teacher, Moses wrote to us and said that if a man dies and leaves a wife but no child, his brother shall marry the widow and have children with her for his brother. Now, there were seven brothers among us. The first brother married, died, leaving no children, and left his wife to his brother. The second brother married her and died, leaving no children. It was the same with the third. Likewise, the same thing happened down to the seventh brother, leaving no children. Last of all, the woman died too. Now, at the resurrection, whose wife of the seven will she be since they all were married to her?"

Jesus answered and said to them, "The people of this world marry and are given in marriage. Those who are considered worthy to obtain that other world and the resurrection of the dead neither marry nor are given in marriage. They cannot die again because they are like the angels. They are sons of God, being sons of the resurrection. You are mistaken because you do not know the Scripture or the power of God. Concerning the resurrection of the dead, even Moses showed that the dead are raised up. Have you not read in the book of Moses what was spoken to you by God in the passage about the burning bush? God spoke to Moses, saying, 'I am the God of Abraham, the God of Isaac, and the God of Jacob.' He is not the God of the dead but of the living—to God all men live; you are badly mistaken." Some of the religion experts said, "Teacher, You have spoken well." After that, no one dared to ask Him any more questions. When the crowd heard this, they were astonished at His teaching.

Important Commands

MATTHEW 22:34–40
MARK 12:28–34

When the Pharisees heard—one of the religion experts heard them disputing with one another and realized He had answered them well—that Jesus had silenced the Sadducees, they gathered together. One of them, one of their religion experts, spoke for them to test Him with a question, saying, "Teacher, which command in God's law is the most important?"

Jesus said, "The most important one is 'Hear, O Israel, the Lord our God is one Lord. You shall love the Lord your God with all your heart, with all your soul, with all your mind, and with all your strength.' This is the first commandment. The second is like it: 'Love your neighbor as yourself.' There is no commandment greater than these, which sum up all the law and prophets."

The religion experts said, "Well said, Teacher! You have said the truth—there is one God and there is no other but Him. To love Him with all your heart, with all your understanding, with all your soul, and with all your strength plus love your neighbor as yourself is more important than all burnt offerings and sacrifices."

When Jesus saw that he answered intelligently, He said to him, "You are not far from the kingdom of God." After that, no one dared ask any more questions.

Whose Son?

MATTHEW 22:41–46
MARK 12:35–37
LUKE 20:41–44

While the Pharisees were still assembled together and while Jesus was teaching in the temple, He asked them, "What do you think about the Christ? Whose Son is He?" They said to Him, "The Son of David."

Jesus said to them, "Then why is it that the religion experts say that the Christ is the Son of David, and why does David, under the inspiration of the Holy Spirit, call Him 'Lord'? David himself states in the book of Psalms:

The Lord said to my Lord:
   'Sit at My right hand
   until I make your enemies your footstool.'

If David himself calls Him, 'Lord,' how can He also be his son?" No one was able to answer Him a word. From that day forth, no one dared to ask Him any more questions. The large crowd listened to Him with delight.

One Rabbi

MATTHEW 23:1–12
MARK 12:38–44
LUKE 20:45—21:4

Then, with all the people listening, Jesus spoke to His disciples, saying, "The religion experts and Pharisees sit in Moses' seat of authority.

Consequently, observe and do everything they tell you, but do not do what they do, because they do not practice what they preach. They tie up heavy loads and place them on men's shoulders, but they themselves are not willing to lift a finger to help. Watch out for the religion experts. All their works are done so they will be noticed by men. They make broad their phylacteries and make long the tassels on their garments. They love to walk around in long robes, receive respectful greetings in the marketplaces, sit in the prominent seats of the synagogue, have places of honor at banquets, and have people call them 'Rabbi.' They devour widows' houses and cover it up by making a show of lengthy prayers. They will receive greater condemnation.

"Nevertheless, you are not to be called 'Rabbi,' because One is your Teacher—Christ—and you are all brothers. Do not call any man on earth your father, because you have One Who is your Father, Who is in heaven. Nor are you to be called 'Teacher,' because One is your Teacher, the Christ. He that is greatest among you will be your servant. Whoever exalts himself will be humbled, and whoever humbles himself will be exalted by others."

Jesus sat near the place where the offerings were placed by the people. He looked up and saw the rich men putting their gifts into the treasury. He also saw a poor widow putting in two mites of copper coins, which are worth less than a cent. Jesus called His disciples to Him and said, "I tell you the truth, this poor widow has put in more than all those who contributed to the treasury. They all gave from the surplus of their abundance, but she gave everything on which she had to live."

You Hypocrites

MATTHEW 23:13–39

Jesus continued, saying, "Woe to you, religion experts and Pharisees. You are hypocrites! You shut the kingdom of heaven in men's faces. You neither enter in yourselves nor do you allow those who are about to enter to go in.

"Woe to you, religion experts and Pharisees. You are hypocrites! You swallow up widows' houses and use the pretense of long prayers to cover it up. You will receive the greater condemnation.

"Woe to you, religion experts and Pharisees. You are hypocrites! You travel over sea and land to make one convert, and when he is converted, then you make him twice as much a child of hell than you are yourselves.

"Woe to you. You are blind guides who say, 'If anyone swears by the temple, it means nothing; but if anyone swears by the gold of the temple, he is bound by his oath.' You blind fools! Which is greater, the gold or the temple that sanctified the gold? You also say, 'Whoever swears by the altar, it means nothing; but whoever swears by the offering on the altar, he is bound by his oath.' You blind fools! Which is greater, the offering or the altar that sanctifies the offering? Hence, whoever swears by the altar swears by it and everything on it. Whoever swears by the temple swears by it and Him Who dwells in it. He who swears by heaven swears by the throne of God and by Him Who sits on it.

"Woe to you, religion experts and Pharisees! You are hypocrites! You tithe your spices—mint, dill, and cumin—and have neglected the more important matters of the law—justice, mercy, and faithfulness. These you should have done without neglecting the others. You blind guides! You strain out a gnat and swallow a camel.

"Woe to you, religion experts and Pharisees. You are hypocrites! You clean the outside of the cup and platter, but inside they are full of extortion and self-indulgence. You blind Pharisees! First clean the inside of the cup and platter so that the outside will also be clean.

"Woe to you, religion experts and Pharisees. You are hypocrites! You are like whitewashed tombs, which appear beautiful on the outside but inside are full of dead men's bones and everything unclean.

"Woe to you, religion experts and Pharisees. You are hypocrites! You build tombs for the prophets and decorate the monuments of the righteous. Then you say, 'If we had lived in the days of our forefathers, we would not have been partakers in shedding the blood of the prophets.' Therefore, you are testifying against yourselves that you are descendants of those who killed the prophets. Fill up, then, the measure of the sin of your fathers.

"You are snakes! You generation of vipers! How can you escape the damnation of hell? Consequently, behold, I am sending you prophets, wise men, and religion experts. Some of them you will kill and crucify. Some of them you will flog in your synagogues and persecute them from town to town. As a result, upon you will come all the righteous blood that has been shed on the earth, from the blood of righteous Abel to the blood of Zechariah, son of Berekiah, whom you murdered between the temple and the altar. I tell you the truth, all these things will come upon this generation.

"O, Jerusalem, Jerusalem, you kill the prophets and stone those who are sent to you! How often I wanted to gather your children together as a hen gathers her chicks under her wings, but you refused Me! Behold, your house is left to you desolate. I say to you, you will not see Me again until you say, 'Blessed is He Who comes in the name of the Lord!'"

Coming Sign

MATTHEW 24:1–14
MARK 13:1–13
LUKE 21:5–19

Some of the people were saying the temple was adorned with beautiful stones and memorial gifts. As Jesus was departing the temple, His disciples came up to Him, pointing out the temple buildings to Him. One of His disciples said to Him, "Teacher, look at the wonderful stones and buildings!" Jesus said, "Do you see all these things? I tell you the truth, the time will come when not one stone will be left on another that will not be torn down."

Later, as Jesus was sitting on the Mount of Olives opposite the temple, His disciples Peter, James, John, and Andrew came to Him privately and said, "Tell us, Teacher, when will these things happen, and what will be the sign that they are about to take place? What will be the sign of Your coming and of the end of the age?"

Jesus answered and said to them, "Be careful that no one deceives you. Many will come in My name and say, 'I am Christ,' and, 'The time is here.' Do not go after them. They will deceive a lot of people. When you hear of wars, rumors of wars, and disturbances, do not be afraid because these things must come to pass first, but the end will not come immediately. Nation will rise against nation and kingdom against kingdom. There will be violent earthquakes in various places, famines, and pestilences. There will be fearful sights and great signs from heaven—this is only the beginning of birth pains.

"Before any of this happens, they will deliver you over to be persecuted and they will kill you—because of Me you will be hated by all nations. At that time many will stumble and fall away from the faith—they will betray and hate each other. Be on your guard. They will deliver you to the courts, you will be beaten in the synagogues, you will be put in prisons, and you will stand before governors and kings because of Me, as a testimony against them. This will be an opportunity for you to witness to them. The Gospel must first be preached to all nations. Therefore, when they arrest you and take you to court, make up your minds not to prepare your defense ahead of time. I will give you words and wisdom that none of your adversaries will be able to stand against or refute. Just say whatever is given you at that time, because it is not you speaking—it is the Holy Spirit. You will be betrayed by parents, brothers, relatives, and friends. Some of you will be put to death—brother will betray brother, father will betray son, and children will rise up against their parents. You will be hated by all men because of Me, but not a hair of your head will perish—by patient endurance you will gain your lives. He who endures to the end will be saved for eternity. Many false prophets will rise up and deceive many people. The increase in wickedness will cause most people's love to grow cold. Again, whoever endures to the end will be saved for eternity. The Gospel of the kingdom will be preached throughout the world as a witness to all nations. Then the end will come."

Abominable Desolation

MATTHEW 24:15–22
MARK 13:14–20
LUKE 21:20–26

Jesus continued, saying, "When you see the abomination of desolation, spoken of by Daniel the prophet, standing where it should not be in the holy place—the temple—" (let the reader understand) "and when you see Jerusalem surrounded by armies, you will know her desolation is near. Then let those who are in Judea flee to the mountains. Let him who is on the housetop not come down to take anything out of the house. Neither let him in the field go back home to get his clothes. Let those in the city get out of it, and do not let those in the country enter the city. Woe to the pregnant women and to nursing mothers! Great misery will be upon the land and wrath against this people. These are days of vengeance in fulfillment of all that has been written of those days. Pray that your flight will not be in the winter or on the Sabbath. The people will be killed by the sword and be led away captive into all nations. Jerusalem will be trampled down by the Gentiles until fulfillment of the Gentile time. There will be signs in the sun, moon, and stars. On the earth there will be anguish of nations. There will be bewilderment at the roaring of the sea and waves, men will faint from fear and expectation of the things that are coming upon the world. The powers of heaven will be shaken loose. In those days will be tribulation that has not been seen since the beginning of the creation that God created until this time—it will never occur again. Except for those days being shortened, no one would survive; however, those days will be shortened for the sake of the elect whom He chose."

Sky Signs

MATTHEW 24:23–35
MARK 13:21–31
LUKE 21:27–33

Jesus continued, saying, "Then if anyone says to you, 'Behold, here is the Christ,' or, 'There He is,' do not believe him. False christs and false prophets will arise, and they will perform great signs and wonders to mislead, if possible, the elect. Behold, I have told you ahead of time.

"So, if they say to you, 'Behold, He is in the desert,' do not go out there, or, 'Behold, He is in the secret chambers,' do not believe it. Just as the lightning comes from the east and can be seen in the west, so also will be the coming of the Son of Man. Wherever there is a carcass, there vultures will gather. Immediately after the tribulation of those days, the sun will darken and the moon will not give her light; the stars will fall from the sky and the powers of the heavens will be shaken!

"Then shall appear the sign of the Son of Man in the sky, and all the nations of the earth will mourn. Then they will see the Son of Man coming on the clouds of the sky with power and great glory. He will send His angels with a loud trumpet call and they will gather His elect from the four winds, from one end of the earth to the ends of heaven. When these things begin to take place, look up and lift up your heads because your redemption is drawing near."

Then He told them a parable, saying, "Look at a fig tree, any tree for that matter, and learn from them. When their branches become tender, bud, and put out their leaves, you see for yourselves and know that summer is near—right at the door. Likewise, when you see these things come to pass, you know that the kingdom of God is near at hand. I tell you the truth, this generation will not pass away until all these things take place. Heaven and earth will pass away, but My words will not pass away."

Keep Watch

MATTHEW 24:36–51
MARK 13:32–37
LUKE 21:34–38

Jesus continued, saying, "However, no one knows that exact day and hour, neither the angels of heaven nor the Son. Only the Father knows. Be on your guard, watch, and pray because you do not know when that time will come. It is like a man taking a journey; he leaves his house and puts his servants in charge, each assigned his work, and commands the doorkeeper to be alert and watch. Therefore, watch because you do not know when the Master of the house will come back—evening, midnight, cockcrowing, or morning. If He comes unexpectedly, do not let Him find you asleep. What I say to you I say to everyone, 'Watch!' As in the days of Noah, so also will be the coming of the Son of Man. Just like the days before the flood, they were eating and drinking, marrying and giving in marriage, until the day Noah entered the ark. They did not know what would happen until the flood came and took them all away—it will be like this with the coming of the Son of Man. Two men will be in the field; one will be taken and the other will be left. Two women will be grinding at the mill; one will be taken and the other left.

"Consequently, watch because you do not know what hour your Lord will return. However, understand this: If the owner of the house knew when the thief would come, he would have watched and would not have allowed his house to be broken into by the thief. Likewise, you be ready, too, because the Son of Man will come at an hour you do not expect Him to return.

"Who, then, is the faithful and wise servant whom his Master has put in charge of His household to give the others their food at the proper time? Blessed is that servant whom his Master finds him doing when He returns. I tell you the truth, He will put him in charge of all His possessions. On the other hand, if that servant is wicked and says to himself, 'My Master is delayed in returning,' and then begins to beat the other servants plus eat and drink with drunkards, the Master of that servant will come on a day and hour he does not expect Him; He will punish him and put him with the hypocrites—there will be weeping and gnashing of teeth.

"Be on your guard so your hearts will not be weighed down with self-indulgence, drunkenness, and the cares of this life to prevent that day from unexpectedly coming on you—it will come on everyone who lives on the face of the entire earth. Watch, therefore, and always pray that you may be accounted worthy to escape all these things that will come to pass and to stand before the Son of Man."

During the day, Jesus taught in the temple and at night He went to the Mount of Olives to spend the night. All the people came early in the morning to the temple to hear Him.

Ten Virgins

MATTHEW 25:1–13

Jesus continued, saying, "Then the kingdom of God will be like ten young virgins who took lamps and went out to meet the bridegroom. Five of them were wise and five were foolish. The foolish ones took their lamps but took no oil for them. The wise ones took oil with them for their lamps. While the bridegroom delayed in coming, they all got drowsy and fell asleep.

"At midnight there was a shout, 'Behold, the bridegroom is here! Go out to meet him!'

"Then the ten virgins got up and trimmed their lamps. The foolish virgins said to the wise ones, 'Give us some of your oil; our lamps have gone out!'

"The wise virgins answered, 'No, there is not enough for both us and you. Instead, go to those who sell oil and buy for yourselves!'

"While they were out buying oil, the bridegroom came, and those who were ready went in with him to the wedding feast. The door was shut.

"Later, the foolish virgins came and said, 'Lord, Lord, open up for us!'

"However, he answered and said, 'I tell you the truth, I do not know you.'

"Therefore, watch because you do not know the day or the hour when the Son of Man will come back."

Faithful Servants

MATTHEW 25:14–30

Jesus continued, saying, "The kingdom of God is like a man, about to travel to a faraway country, who called his servants and entrusted his property to them. To one he gave five talents" (about five thousand dollars), "to another two talents, and to another one talent—to every man according to his ability. Then he departed on his journey. The servant who received the five talents went and traded with them and gained five more talents. Likewise, the servant who had received two talents gained two more talents. However, the servant who received one talent went and dug a hole in the ground to hide his master's money.

"After a long time, the master of those servants came back and settled accounts with them. The one given five talents came and brought him five more, saying, 'Master, you entrusted me with five talents and I have gained five talents more.'

"His master said to him, 'Well done, you good and faithful servant! You have been faithful over a few things; I will put you in charge of many things. Enter into the joy of your master!'

"The servant who was given the two talents came and said, 'Master, you entrusted me with two talents and I have gained two talents more!'

"His master said to him, 'Well done, you good and faithful servant! You have been faithful over a few things; I will put you in charge of many things! Enter into the joy of your master!'

"Then the servant given one talent came and said, 'Master, I knew that you are a hard man, reaping where you have not sown and gathering where you did not scatter seed. I was afraid, so I went and hid your talent in the ground. See, here is your talent!'

"His master said to him, 'You wicked and lazy servant! You knew I harvest where I have not sown and gather where I have not scattered seed. You should have at least put my money in the bank, and at my coming I could have received my money back with interest.

"'Take the talent from him and give it to the servant with ten talents. To everyone who has shall be given more and he will have abundance. However, from him who does not have, even what he has will be taken from him. Cast the worthless servant into the outer darkness where there will be weeping and gnashing of teeth.'"

Separating Sheep

MATTHEW 25:31–46

Jesus continued, saying, "When the Son of Man arrives in His glory, accompanied with the holy angels, then He will sit on the throne of His glory. All nations will gather before Him, and He will separate the people one from another as a shepherd divides his sheep from the goats. He will put the sheep at His right but the goats at His left.

"Then the King will say to those on His right, 'Come, you who are blessed by My Father. Inherit the kingdom prepared for you from the foundation of the world. This is because I was hungry and you fed Me; I was thirsty and you gave Me something to drink; I was a stranger and you asked Me in; I was naked and you gave Me clothes; I was sick and you visited Me; I was in prison and you came to see Me.'

"Then those righteous sheep will say, 'Lord, when did we see You hungry and feed You or see You thirsty and give You something to drink? When did we see You a stranger and ask You in or see You naked and give You clothes? When did we see You sick or in prison and come to visit You?'

"The King will reply to them, saying, 'I tell you the truth, when you did it to one of the least of these brothers of Mine, you did it to Me.'

Then He will turn to the goats on His left and say, 'Depart from Me, you cursed ones, into eternal fire that is prepared for the devil and his angels, because I was hungry and you did not feed Me; I was thirsty and you gave Me nothing to drink; I was a stranger and you did not ask Me in; I was naked and you gave Me no clothes; I was sick and in prison but you did not come to see Me.'

"Then those on the left will answer Him, saying, 'Lord, when did we see You hungry, thirsty, a stranger, naked, sick, or in prison and not minister to You?'

"Then He will answer them, saying, 'I tell you the truth, when you failed to do these things for the least of these, you failed to do it for Me.'

"Then those on His left will go to eternal punishment, but the righteous will go to eternal life."

Death Fruit

JOHN 12:20–36a

There were some Greeks among those who had come up to worship at the Feast. They came to Philip, who was from Bethsaida in Galilee, with a request, saying, "Sir, we want to see Jesus." Philip went and told Andrew. Then Andrew and Philip went and told Jesus.

Jesus answered them, saying, "The hour has come for the glorification of the Son of Man. I tell you the truth, unless a grain of wheat falls to the ground and dies, it remains a lone grain. On the other hand, if it is buried, it produces much fruit. Anyone who loves his life will lose it, but anyone who hates his life in this world will keep it to life eternal. If anyone wants to serve Me, he must follow Me. Where I am, there will My servant be also. If anyone serves Me, My Father will honor him.

"Right now My soul is troubled and what shall I say? 'Father, save Me from this hour?' No, this is the reason I came to this hour. Father, glorify Your name!"

Then there came a voice from heaven, saying, "I have glorified it and will glorify it again." The crowd of bystanders heard it and said it had thundered, while others said an angel had spoken to Him.

Jesus answered and said, "The voice did not come for My sake but for your sakes. Now judgment is upon this world. Now the prince of this world will be cast out. When I am lifted up from the earth, I will attract all men to Me." He said this to show how He was going to be put to death.

The crowd answered, "We heard from the law that the Christ lasts forever. Why, then, do You say, 'The Son of Man will be lifted up'? Who is this 'Son of Man'?"

So Jesus said to them, "For a brief time longer the Light will be among you. Walk while you have the Light so that darkness does not overtake you. He who walks in the darkness does not know where he is going. While you have the Light, believe in the Light so you may become sons of Light."

Judging Words

JOHN 12:36b–50

After saying these things, Jesus departed and hid Himself from them. Even though He performed many miracles before them, they still did not believe in Him. This fulfilled what the prophet Isaiah said:

Lord, who believes our message?
To whom has been revealed the arm of the Lord?

As a result, they could not believe because Isaiah also said:

He has blinded their eyes
    and hardened their hearts
to keep them from seeing with their eyes
    and understanding with their hearts
and be converted
    or turning to Me to heal them.

Isaiah said these things when he saw God's glory and spoke to Him.

Nevertheless, many of the chief rulers believed in Him. However, because of the Pharisees, they did not confess their belief because they were afraid of being put out of the synagogue—they loved the praise of men more than the praise of God.

Jesus cried out and said, "Whoever believes in Me believes not just in Me but in the One Who sent Me. Whoever sees Me sees the One Who sent Me. I came as a Light into the world so that whoever believes in Me does not remain in the darkness.

"If anyone hears My words and does not keep them, I do not judge him. I did not come to judge the world; I came to save the world. Those who reject Me and refuse to accept My teachings have One Who judges them—the Word I have spoken will judge them in the last day. This is because I did not speak of My own authority, but the Father Who sent Me commanded Me what I should say and how to say it. I know that His commandment leads to eternal life. So, whatever I speak is what the Father has told Me to say."

Burial Perfume

MATTHEW 26:1–16
MARK 14:1–11
LUKE 22:1–6

The Feast of Unleavened Bread, also called the Feast of Passover, drew near—it was two days before their start. When Jesus finished saying these things, He said to His disciples, "You know that the Feast of Passover is in two days, and that is when the Son of Man will be betrayed for crucifixion."

Then the chief priests, religion experts, and elders of the people assembled together in the palace of the high priest, whose name was Caiaphas. They consulted together to subtly take Jesus—they feared the people—and kill Him. They said, "We should not do it during the Feast of Passover because there may be a riot among the people.

When Jesus was in Bethany, in the house of Simon the leper, a woman came up to Him as He sat eating; she had a vial of very expensive perfume of pure nard. She broke the vial and poured it on His head.

When the disciples and some of the guests saw this happen, they were saying indignantly among themselves, "Why this waste of perfume? It could have been sold for a great deal of money, and the money could have been given to the poor." They were scolding her.

Jesus was aware of what was going on and said to them, "Why are you bothering the woman? She has done something praiseworthy for Me. You will always have the poor with you, and whenever you desire you do them good, but you will not always have Me with you. She has done what she could. When she poured this perfume on My body, she did it to prepare Me for burial. I tell you the truth, wherever this Gospel is preached in the whole world, what this woman has done will be told also in memory of her."

Then Satan entered one of the Twelve named Judas Iscariot. He left and went to the chief priests and temple guards; he discussed with them how he might betray Jesus to them. He asked, "What will you give me if I hand Him over to you?" When they heard this, they were delighted and promised to give him money. They paid him thirty pieces of silver. From then on, Judas sought an opportunity to betray Him away from the crowd.

Passover Meal

MATTHEW 26:17–25
MARK 14:12–21
LUKE 22:7–13; 22:21–23
JOHN 13:1–2; 13:18–30

Just before the Feast of Passover, Jesus knew that His time had come to depart this world to go to the Father. He loved His own who were in the world; He loved them to the end.

The first day of Unleavened Bread came when the Passover lamb was to be sacrificed on the altar. On this day the disciples came to Jesus and asked, "Where do You want us to go and prepare so You can eat the Passover meal?"

Jesus sent two of His disciples, Peter and John, saying, "Go prepare the Passover meal for us so we can eat it." They asked Him, "Where do You want us to prepare the meal?" Jesus said, "Behold, when you enter the city, you will meet a man carrying a jug of water. Follow him to the house he goes inside. Go to the owner of that house and say, 'The Teacher wants to know: "Where is My guest room where I can eat the Passover meal with My disciples?" He also says, "My time is near. I and My disciples will celebrate the Passover meal at your house."' He will show you a large upstairs room that is furnished and ready. Prepare the meal there." The disciples followed Jesus' instructions—they left, went into the city, and found everything just as He had told them—and prepared the Passover meal.

When it was evening, Jesus arrived with the Twelve. During the meal, they were reclining at the table. Satan had already put the thought of betraying Him into the heart of Judas Iscariot, Simon's son. While they were eating, Jesus said, "I tell you the truth, one of you who is eating with Me will betray Me. I am not speaking of all of you; I know those whom I have chosen. Nevertheless, this is to fulfill Scripture, which says, 'He who eats bread with Me has lifted up his heel against Me.' I am telling you all this before it occurs so that when it does take place, you will believe that I am Who I say I am. I tell you the truth, whoever accepts Me accepts the One Who sent Me."

After He said these things, Jesus became troubled in spirit and said, "I tell you the truth, one of you is going to betray Me."

The disciples looked at each other, wondering who He was talking about. They were deeply saddened and each of them, one by one, said, "Lord, surely it is not I." They began to ask each other which of them would do this thing.

Jesus answered them, saying, "It is one of you Twelve who dips bread with Me in the bowl who will betray Me. The Son of Man goes as it is written of Him, but woe to the man who betrays the Son of Man! It would have been better for that man if he was never born."

One of the disciples, the one Jesus loved, was leaning on His bosom. Simon Peter gestured to this disciple to ask Jesus who He meant. He leaned back and asked, "Lord, who is it?" Jesus answered, "It is the one to whom I am going to give this piece of bread after I have dipped it." When He dipped it, He gave it to Judas Iscariot, the son of Simon. After he took the bread, Satan entered into him.

Then Judas, who betrayed him, asked, "Master, surely it is not I, is it?"

Jesus said to him, "Yes, you have said it."

Then Jesus said to Judas Iscariot, "What you are going to do, do it quickly." No one at the table knew why Jesus said this to him. Some thought that since Judas was their treasurer, Jesus was telling him to buy what they needed for the Feast or that he should give something to the poor.

After receiving the piece of bread, Judas left immediately. It was night.

Jesus Gives

MATTHEW 26:26–29
MARK 14:22–25
LUKE 22:14–20; 22:24–30

When it was time, Jesus reclined at the table with His apostles and said, "I have eagerly desired to eat this Passover meal with you before I enter My time of suffering, because, I tell you, I will never eat it again until it is fulfilled in the kingdom of God."

While they were eating, Jesus took bread, blessed it, broke it, and gave it to His disciples, saying, "Take it, divide it among yourselves, and eat it. This is My body which is given for you. Do this in remembrance of Me." Then, after the meal, He likewise took the cup, gave thanks, and gave it to them, saying, "Take this and divide it among yourselves. Drink from it, all of you." They all drank from it. Then He said, "This is My blood of the new covenant, which I shed for you and many others for the forgiveness of sins. I tell you, I will not drink again of this fruit of the vine until the day I drink it new with you in My Father's kingdom."

There also arose a dispute among them as to which of them would be considered the greatest. Jesus intervened, saying, "The Gentile kings exercise lordship over them, and those in authority over them are called benefactors. However, this shall not be so with you, because he who is the greatest among you, let him be like the servant. Who is greater, the one who reclines at the table or the one who serves? Is it not the one who reclines at the table? Nevertheless, I am among you as One Who serves. You are those who have remained with Me through My trials. I confer on you a kingdom just as My Father conferred one on Me, so that you may eat and drink at My table in My kingdom and sit on thrones judging the twelve tribes of Israel."

Washing Feet

JOHN 13:3–17

Jesus knew that the Father had put everything under His power, that He came from God and that He was returning to God. He got up from the table, laid aside His garments, and, taking a towel, girded His waist. Then He poured water into a basin and began to wash the disciples' feet, drying them with the towel that girded His waist.

Then He came to Simon Peter, who said, "Lord, is it Your place to wash my feet?"

Jesus replied to him, "You do not understand now what I am doing, but you will understand hereafter."

Peter said to Him, "You shall never wash my feet."

Jesus answered him, saying, "If I do not wash you, you have no part with Me."

Simon Peter said to Him, "Lord, wash not only my feet but also my hands and head, too!"

Jesus said, "He who has washed does not need to wash anything except his feet to be clean all over. You, My disciples, are clean but not all of you." He said this because He knew who was His betrayer—that was the reason He said not everyone was clean.

When He finished washing their feet, He put on His garments and sat down again. Then He said, "Do you understand what I have done to you? You call Me Teacher, and rightly so, because that is what I am! If I then, your Lord and Teacher, washed your feet, you also ought to wash each other's feet. I have given you an example—you should do as I have done for you. I tell you the truth, the servant is not greater than his master, nor is anyone who is sent—the messenger—superior to the one who sent him. If you know these things, you will be happy if you do them."

New Commandment

JOHN 13:31–35

Jesus said (Judas Iscariot had already left), "Now is the Son of Man glorified and God is glorified through Him. If God is glorified through Him, God will also glorify Him in Himself and will glorify Him immediately.

"Little children, I am with you for only a short time longer. You will seek Me, and, as I said to the Jews, I now tell you, 'Where I go, you are not able to come.'

"I give you a new commandment: Love one another. In the same way I loved you, so you must love one another. This is how all men will know that you are My disciples, if you have love for each other."

Satan's Demand

MATTHEW 26:30–35
MARK 14:26–31
LUKE 22:31–39
JOHN 13:36–38

When they had sung a hymn, they went to the Mount of Olives.

Simon Peter asked, "Lord, where are You going?"

Jesus answered, "You cannot now follow Me where I am going, but you will follow Me later."

Peter asked Him, "Why can I not follow You now? I will lay down my life for You."

Then Jesus said to them, "Tonight, all of you will fall away because of Me. It is written:

I will strike down the Shepherd,
and the sheep of the flock shall be scattered abroad.

In spite of this, after I am raised up, I will go ahead of you to Galilee."

The Lord said, "Simon, Simon, behold, Satan has demanded permission to sift you like wheat. However, I have prayed especially for you that your faith may not fail. When you have turned back, strengthen your brothers."

Peter said to Him, "Lord, I am ready to go with You both to prison and to death. Even if all others fall away because of You, I never will do so."

Jesus said, "Will you lay down your life for Me? I tell you the truth, tonight, Peter, before the rooster crows twice, you will deny three times that you know Me."

Peter vehemently said, "Even if I had to die with You, I would never deny You!" All the other disciples said the same thing.

Then Jesus said to them, "When I sent you out without a money purse, bag of provisions, or sandals, did you lack anything?"

They said, "No, we lacked nothing."

Then Jesus said, "Now it is different. If you have a money purse, take it. Also take a bag of provisions. If you do not have a sword, sell your robe and buy one. I tell you that what is written, 'He was wanted among the wicked,' must be fulfilled in Me."

They said, "Lord, behold, we have two swords."

Jesus said, "That is enough."

Jesus' Way

John 14:1–14

Jesus continued, saying, "Do not let this trouble your hearts. You trust God, trust Me, also. In My Father's house are many dwelling places. If that were not so, would I have told you I am going there to prepare a place for you? Also, if I go there to prepare a place for you, I will come back to take you to be with Me so that where I am you will be also—you know where I am going and you know how to get there."

Thomas said to Him, "Lord, we do not know where You are going, so how can You say we know the way?"

Jesus said, "I am the way, the truth, and the life. No one comes to the Father except through Me. If you had known Me, you would have known My Father also. From now on, you know Him and have seen Him."

Philip said, "Lord, show us the Father; that will satisfy us."

Jesus responded, "You have been with Me all this time, Philip, and you still do not know Me? Anyone who sees Me sees the Father. So how can you ask, 'Show us the Father'? Do you not believe that I am in the Father and the Father is in Me? The words that I speak to you are not on My own authority. It is the Father Who resides in Me doing His work. Believe Me that I am in the Father and the Father is in Me. At least believe in the miracles I perform in My Father's name. I tell you the truth, anyone who believes in Me will not only be able to do what I do but even greater things than these because I go to the Father. I will do whatever you ask in My name so that the Father will be glorified through the Son. Anything you ask in My name I will do it."

Love Obeys

JOHN 14:15–24

Jesus said to His disciples, "If you love Me, you will keep My commandments. I will ask the Father and He will give you another Comforter to be with you forever. He is the Spirit of Truth, Whom the world cannot accept because it does not see Him nor does it know Him. However, you know Him because He dwells with you and will even be in you. In just a little while the world will no longer see Me, but you are going to see Me; because I live, you will live also. On that day you will know that I am in My Father, that you are in Me and that I am in you. The person who knows My commandments and keeps them is the one who loves Me. The person who loves Me will be loved by My Father; I will also love him and will disclose Myself to him."

Then Judas (not Iscariot) said, "Lord, how will You disclose Yourself to us but not to the world?"

Jesus replied, "If anyone loves Me, he will obey My teaching and My Father will love him. We will come to him and make Our home with him. Anyone who does not love Me does not obey My teaching. The words you hear are not Mine—they come from the Father Who sent Me."

Bear Fruit

JOHN 14:25—15:17

Jesus continued, saying, "I am telling you these things while I am still living with you. The Comforter, which is the Holy Spirit Whom the Father will send in My name, will teach you all things and will enable you to remember everything I have said to you. Peace I leave with you;

My peace I give to you, but not as the world gives to you. Do not let your heart be troubled nor let it be afraid either.

"You heard Me tell you, 'I am going away and I am coming back to you.' If you loved Me, you would rejoice because I am going to the Father, Who is greater than I. Before it occurs, I have told you so that when it does happen you will believe in Me more deeply. Hereafter, I will not talk with you much because the prince of the world is coming. He has no power over Me. However, so that the world may know that I love the Father, I obey what He commands Me.

"Arise, let us leave here.

"I am the true Vine and My Father is the Vinedresser. He cuts off every branch in Me that does not bear fruit. He prunes every branch that bears fruit so it will bear more fruit. You are already clean and pruned because of the teachings I have given you. Dwell in Me and I will dwell in you. Just as the branch cannot bear fruit by itself without remaining on the vine, neither can you bear fruit unless you are joined with Me.

"I am the Vine; you are the branches. Whoever lives in Me and I in him bears much fruit. You can do nothing apart from Me. Anyone who does not dwell in Me is thrown away as a separated branch and withers. These branches are gathered up and thrown into the fire to be burned up. If you live in Me and My words live in you, ask what you desire and it shall be done for you. My Father is glorified when you bear much fruit—you prove yourselves to be My disciples.

"Just as the Father has loved Me, I likewise have loved you. Continue in My love. If you obey My commandments, you will remain in My love, just as I have obeyed My Father's commandments and remain in His love. I have told you these things so that My joy might be in you and so that your joy may be full. My command is that you love one another the way I loved you. No one has greater love than to lay down his life for his friends. You are My friends if you do the things I command you. I am no longer calling you servants because servants do not know what their master is doing; I have called you friends because I have told you everything I have heard from My Father. You did not choose Me; I chose you and put you in the world to bear fruit that will last so that whatever you ask of the Father in My name, He will give you. This is My command to you: love one another."

World Hate

JOHN 15:18—16:4a

Jesus continued, saying, "If the world hates you, know that it hated Me before it hated you. If you belonged to the world, the world would love you as one of its own. However, you are not of the world because I have chosen you out of the world. For that reason, the world hates you. Remember the words I said to you: 'The servant is not greater than his Master.' If they persecuted Me, they will also persecute you. If they obeyed My teaching, they will also obey yours. They will treat you this way because of My name and because they do not know the One Who sent Me. If I had not come and spoken to them, they would not be guilty of sin. Nevertheless, now they have no excuse for their sin. Whoever hates Me hates My Father also. If I had not done among them things which no one else has ever done, they would not be guilty of sin. However, now they have both seen these miracles and have hated both Me and My Father. This came to pass so that the word written in the law might be fulfilled: 'They hated Me without cause.'

"When the Counselor comes, Whom I will send to you from the Father—the Spirit of Truth Who proceeds from the Father—He will testify regarding Me. You also will and must testify about Me because you have been with Me from the beginning.

"I have told you these things so that you do not fall away. They are going to throw you out of the synagogues, and there will even come a time when anyone who kills you will think he is doing a service to God. They will do these things to you because they have not known the

Father or Me. I have told you these things so that when the time comes you will remember that I told you of them."

Comforter Sent

JOHN 16:4b–16

Jesus continued, saying, "I did not tell you this at the beginning because I was with you. Now I am going to Him Who sent Me, yet none of you asks Me, 'Where are You going?' Because I have said these things to you, sorrow has filled your heart. Nevertheless, I tell you the truth, it is to your advantage that I go away, because if I do not leave, the Comforter will not come to you. On the other hand, if I go, I will send Him to you. When He comes, He will convict the world about sin, righteousness, and judgment—about sin because of their refusal to believe in Me; about righteousness because I go to the Father and you will see Me no more; about judgment because the prince of this world has been judged already.

"I still have many more things to tell you, but you cannot bear them now. However, when He, the Spirit of Truth, comes, He will speak on His own authority but only what He hears from the Father. He will speak to you and He will tell you what will happen in the future. He will glorify Me by taking what is Mine and make it known to you.

"In a little while you are not going to see Me, but then, in a little while, you will see Me."

My Name

JOHN 16:17–33

Then some of His disciples said among themselves, "What does He mean when He says, 'In a little while you are not going to see Me, but then, in a little while, you will see Me,' and, 'because I am going to the Father'?" They said, "What does He mean when He says, 'in a little while'? We do not understand what He is talking about."

Jesus knew they wanted to ask Him what He meant, so He said to them, "Are you wondering among yourselves what I meant when I said, 'In a little while you are not going to see Me, but then, in a little while, you will see Me'? I tell you the truth, you will weep and mourn, but the world will rejoice. You will be sorrowful, but your sorrow will turn into joy. A woman giving birth is in pain because her time has come, but when she delivers the child, she no longer remembers the pain because she is joyful a child has been born into the world. Likewise, you are sorrowful now, but I will see you again and your heart will rejoice. No one will be able to take away your joy. In that day, you will no longer have questions for Me. I tell you the truth, whatever you ask the Father in My name, He will give it to you. Until now, you have not asked anything in My name. Ask and you will receive so that your joy will be full.

"These things I have spoken to you in figurative language, but the time is coming when I will no longer speak to you in figurative language—I will tell you plainly about the Father. Then you will ask in My name. I am not saying I will ask the Father on your behalf; this will not be necessary because the Father Himself loves you because you have loved Me and have believed that I came from the Father. I came from the Father and came into the world. Now I am going to leave the world and go to the Father."

His disciples said, "Finally You are speaking plainly and not in figurative language; there is no need to ask You questions. By this we are convinced You came from God."

Jesus answered them, "Do you finally believe? In fact, the hour is coming and has already come when you will be scattered, every man to his own home, leaving Me alone. Yet I am not alone because the Father is with Me.

"I have told you these things so that in Me you may have peace. In this world you will have trials, but be of good cheer—I have overcome the world."

Jesus Prays

JOHN 17:1–26

When Jesus had said these things, He lifted His eyes to heaven and said:

"Father, the time has come. Glorify Your Son so that Your Son may glorify You. You have given Him authority over all mankind so that He may give eternal life to all You have given Him. This is eternal life: that they know You, the only true God, and Jesus Christ, Whom You have sent to earth. I have glorified You on the earth by finishing the work You gave Me to do on earth. Now, Father, glorify Me and Yourself with the glory that I had with You before the beginning of the world.

"I have revealed Your name to the men You gave Me out of the world. They were Yours, You gave them to Me, and they have obeyed Your Word. Now they understand that everything You have given Me is from You. I have given them the words that You gave Me, they have accepted them, believe that I came from You, and believe that You sent Me. I pray for them. I am not praying for the world but for those You gave Me because they belong to You. All I have is Yours and all You have is Mine. I am glorified through them. Now I am no longer remaining in the world, but they are in the world, and I am returning to You. Holy Father, protect in Your name those whom You have given Me so that they may be one as We are One. While I was with them in the world, I kept them safe in Your name. Those whom You gave Me I have protected, and none of them has been lost except the son of perdition in fulfillment of the Scripture.

"Now I am returning to You. I speak these things while I am still in the world so that My joy may be completed in them. I have given them Your Word, and the world has hated them because they do not belong to the world, even as I am not of the world. I do not pray that You will take them out of the world but that You will protect them from the evil one. They do not belong to the world even as I am not of the world. Sanctify them by Your truth—Your Word is truth. Just like You sent Me into the world, I have also sent them into the world. For their sakes I sanctify Myself so that they might also be sanctified through the truth.

"I am praying not only for them but also for those who will believe in Me through their teaching, so that they all may be one in Us and so that the world may believe that You sent Me. The glory that You have given Me I have given to them so that they may be one even as We are One. I in them and You in Me, so they may have perfect unity so that the world may recognize that You have sent Me and that You have loved them as You have loved Me.

"Father, I desire that those You gave Me may be with Me where I am so they may see My glory, which You have given to Me. You loved Me before the creation of the world.

"Righteous Father, the world has not recognized You, but I have known You. These men know that You have sent Me. I have revealed to them Your name—Who You are—and will continue to make You known so that the love You have for Me may be in them and that I may be in them."

Gethsemane Agony

MATTHEW 26:36–46
MARK 14:32–42
LUKE 22:40–46
JOHN 18:1

Jesus, having prayed this prayer, left with His disciples, crossed the brook Kidron, and entered a garden area called Gethsemane. When they arrived there, Jesus said to His disciples, "Pray that you do not give in to temptation. Sit here while I pray." He took with Him Peter and the two sons of Zebedee, James and John. He became sorrowfully distressed to a great degree. Then He said to them, "My soul is exceedingly sorrowful even to the point of death. Stay here and keep watch with Me."

He went a stone's throw farther away from them, fell to the ground, kneeling, and prayed that, if it were possible, the hour might pass from Him. He said, "Abba, Father, everything is possible for You. If it is possible, let this cup pass away from Me. Nevertheless, not what I will but what You will." There appeared an angel from heaven to Him, strengthening Him. Being in agony, He prayed more earnestly. His sweat was like great drops of blood falling to the ground.

When He came back to His disciples, He found them asleep. He said to Peter, "Simon, are you asleep? Could you not keep watch for one hour? Watch and pray so that you do not fall into temptation. The spirit is truly willing, but the flesh is weak."

He went away again a second time and prayed the same thing, saying, "My Father, if this cup cannot pass away from Me unless I drink it, Your will be done."

He returned again and found them asleep. They simply could not keep their eyes open, and they did not know what to say to Him. He left them and went away again to pray the third time, saying the same thing.

He got up from prayer, and, when He came back a third time to the disciples and found them asleep, because of their sorrow, He said, "Why are you sleeping and resting? It is enough! The hour has come and the Son of Man is betrayed into the hands of sinners. Get up! Pray that you do not enter into temptation. Let us go! My betrayer is at hand!"

Dark Night

MATTHEW 26:47–56
MARK 14:43–52
LUKE 22:47–53
JOHN 18:2–11

Immediately, while Jesus was still speaking, Judas, one of the Twelve, showed up leading a crowd of Roman soldiers and guards sent by the chief priests, religion experts, Pharisees, and elders of the Sanhedrin.

(Judas, His betrayer, knew the place because Jesus and His disciples went there often.) They came with lanterns and torches; they were armed with swords and clubs. Jesus, knowing everything that was going to befall Him, went out to them and asked, "Whom do you seek?" They answered, "Jesus of Nazareth." Jesus said to them, "I am He." Judas, His betrayer, was standing with them. When Jesus said, "I am He," they drew back and fell to the ground. Jesus asked again, "Whom do you seek?" They answered, "Jesus of Nazareth." Jesus answered, "I told you that I am He. If, therefore, you seek Me, let these men go their way." This fulfilled when He spoke, saying, "Those whom You gave Me I have protected and none of them has been lost." Now the betrayer had worked out a sign with them, saying, "The One I kiss, that is the One. Seize Him and lead Him away under guard." Judas went straight to Jesus and said, "Greetings, Master!" and approached Jesus to kiss Him.

However, Jesus said, "Judas, are you going to betray the Son of Man with a kiss? Friend, why are you here?"

Then they laid their hands on Him and arrested Him. When those with Him saw what was happening, they said, "Lord, shall we fight with the sword?" Just then Simon Peter, one of the men standing there with Jesus who had a sword, reached and drew out his sword. He struck the high priest's servant—his name was Malchus—and cut off his right ear. Jesus said, "Let them do this to Me!" Then, touching the servant's ear, He healed him.

Then Jesus said to Peter, "Put your sword back where it belongs. All who draw the sword will perish by the sword. Do you not know that I can pray to My Father and He would immediately give Me more than twelve legions of angels? However, if I did that, how would Scriptures be fulfilled that say it must happen this way? The cup that My Father has given Me, shall I not drink it?"

At that moment, Jesus addressed the crowd (the chief priests, officers of the temple guard, and elders of the Sanhedrin), saying, "Have you come as if I was a thief, with swords and clubs to arrest Me? Daily I sat with you teaching in the temple and you did not arrest Me. Nevertheless, this is your hour and the powers of darkness are yours. All this has taken place to fulfill the Scriptures of the prophets." Then all His disciples deserted Him and fled from Him. A young man followed Jesus with nothing but a linen garment over his naked body. When they grabbed him, he escaped from them naked, leaving the linen garment behind.

Before Annas

MATTHEW 26:58; 26:69–70
MARK 14:54; 14:66–68
LUKE 22:54–57
JOHN 18:12–24

Then the Roman soldiers, with their commander and the Jewish guards, seized Jesus and bound Him. They led Him away and brought Him to the house of the high priest, where the religion experts and elders were gathered together. They took Him first to Annas, father-in-law of Caiaphas, who was high priest that year. Caiaphas was the one who had advised the Jews that it was expedient for one man to die for the people.

Simon Peter and another disciple followed Jesus at a distance until they got to the courtyard of the high priest's house. That other disciple was known to the high priest; as a result, he went with Jesus into the high priest's courtyard, but Peter had to stand outside at the door. Then the other disciple, who was known by the high priest, went out and spoke to the servant girl who was the doorkeeper and brought Peter inside. When Peter was inside, he sat with the guards to see the outcome.

Since it was cold, the servants and guards kindled a fire in the middle of the courtyard. They sat down together by it to warm themselves. Peter sat down and stood with them to get warm. Meanwhile, Annas questioned Jesus regarding His disciples and His teaching. Jesus answered him, saying, "I spoke openly in public. I have taught regularly in the synagogue and in the temple where the Jews come together. I spoke nothing in secret. Why do you question Me? Ask those who heard what I said to them."

When He said this, one of the guards standing there struck Jesus, saying, "Is that how you are to speak to the high priest?"

Jesus replied, "If I have said anything wrong, tell Me what I said wrong. On the other hand, if I spoke truthfully, why did you strike Me?"

Then Annas sent Him, still tied up, to Caiaphas the high priest.

All this time, Peter was sitting down below in the courtyard. A servant girl of the high priest came in and, when she saw Peter warming himself as he sat by the fire, came up to him, looking at him intently, and said, "This man also was with Him. You also were with Jesus the Galilean of Nazareth."

Peter denied it before all of them, saying, "I am not. I do not know or understand what you are talking about. Woman, I do not know Him." Then he went out to the porch and a cock crowed immediately.

Before Caiaphas

MATTHEW 26:57; 26:59–68
MARK 14:53; 14:55–65
LUKE 22:63–71

Those who had arrested Jesus led Him away to Caiaphas the high priest, where all the chief priests, religion experts, and elders had assembled together.

As soon as it was daylight, the elders of the people—the elders of the Sanhedrin, chief priests, and religion experts—came together and they led Jesus before their council, where they tried to obtain false witnesses to testify against Him so they could put Him to death. They did not find any. Many falsely testified against Jesus, but their statements did not agree.

Finally, two men stood up, came forward, and gave false testimony against Jesus, saying, "We heard Him say, 'I am able to, and will, destroy the temple of God made with hands, and in three days I will build another one not made by man.'" Still, not even in this did their testimony agree.

The high priest stood up in their midst and spoke to Jesus, asking, "Are You not going to answer? What do You have to say about the testimony of these men against You?"

Jesus kept silent and made no reply.

Again, the high priest said to Him, "Are You the Christ, the Son of the Blessed—the Son of God? I command You to tell us by the living God."

Jesus said to them, "If I tell you, you will not believe Me, and if I question you, you will not answer Me nor let Me go. From here on the Son of Man will sit at the right hand of power of God."

Jesus continued, saying, "Yes, I am. Nevertheless, I tell you, hereafter you will see the Son of Man sitting at the right hand of power of God and coming on the clouds of heaven."

Then the high priest tore his clothes, saying, "What need do we have of any further witnesses? He has blasphemed! You have heard the blasphemy from His own mouth!"

They all condemned Him of being guilty and deserving death, saying, "He deserves to be put to death."

Then some of the men guarding Jesus began mocking Him, beat Him, and spit on His face. Others slapped Him on the face. They covered His face and struck Him with their fists, saying, "Prophesy to us, You Christ. Who struck You?" They said many other blasphemous things to Him. The guards punched and slapped Him as they took Him away.

Peter's Denial

MATTHEW 26:71–75
MARK 14:69–72
LUKE 22:58–62
JOHN 18:25–27

Meanwhile, Simon Peter was at the fire warming himself. As he moved over toward the porch, another servant girl saw him. She began saying to those standing there, "This man also is one of them. This fellow also was with Jesus of Nazareth." Then she said to Peter, "Are you not also one of His disciples?"

Again he denied it with an oath, saying, "I am not! I do not know the Man!"

After a little while, about an hour later, someone else of the bystanders, one of the high priest's servants who was a relative of the man whose ear Peter had cut off, approached Peter, emphatically saying, "Did I not see you in the garden with Him? Surely you are one of them. Your accent betrays you—you are a Galilean."

Then Peter began to curse and he swore to them, saying, "I do not know the Man! I do not know what you are talking about! I do not know this Man you are talking about!"

Immediately, the cock crowed a second time. Just then, the Lord turned and looked at Peter. Then he remembered what the Lord Jesus had said to him: "Before the rooster crows twice, you will deny Me three times." When Peter thought about it, he went out and wept bitterly.

Blood Money

MATTHEW 27:1–10
MARK 15:1
LUKE 23:1
JOHN 18:28a

Early in the morning, the chief priests consulted with the elders, religion experts, and the entire Sanhedrin council. They bound Jesus, led Him away from Caiaphas, and delivered Him to the palace of Pontius Pilate, the Roman governor.

Then Judas, the one who betrayed Jesus, when he saw that He was condemned, was remorseful and returned the thirty silver coins to the high priests and elders, saying, "I have sinned—I have betrayed innocent blood."

They said, "What is that to us? That is your problem."

Judas threw down the silver coins in the temple and left; then he went out and hanged himself.

The high priests picked up the silver pieces, saying, "It is not lawful to put them in the temple treasury because it is the price of blood." So, after consulting each other, they used the money to buy the potter's field in which to bury strangers. Therefore, that field has been called the Field of Blood to this day. This fulfilled what was spoken by the prophet Jeremiah when he said, "They took the thirty pieces of silver, the price of Him that was determined by the children of Israel. They gave the money for the potter's field, as the Lord directed me."

Before Pilate

MATTHEW 27:11–31
MARK 15:2–20
LUKE 23:2–25
JOHN 18:28b—19:16

Jesus now stood before Pilate, the governor. The Jews did not enter the palace because they did not want to be defiled and, therefore, unable to eat the Passover. So Pilate came out to them and said, "What accusation do you bring against this Man?"

They replied, "If He was not a criminal, we would not have handed Him over to you."

Pilate said to them, "Take Him yourselves and judge Him according to your law."

The Jews said, "It is not lawful for us to put any man to death." This fulfilled what Jesus spoke signifying the way He would die.

The chief priests accused Him of many things, saying, "We found this Man misleading our nation and forbidding taxes to be paid to Caesar, saying He is Christ, a king." Still Jesus said nothing.

Pilate went back into the palace again, called for Jesus, and asked Him, "Are You the 'King of the Jews'?"

Jesus answered, "It is as you say. Are you saying this on your own, or did others tell you this about Me?"

Pilate said, "Am I a Jew? Your own people and the chief priests have turned You over to me. What have You done?"

Jesus answered, "My kingdom is not of this world. If My kingdom was of this world, My servants would fight so that I would not be handed over to the Jews. However, My kingdom is not of this world."

Then Pilate said, "So, are You a king?"

Jesus answered, "You say correctly that I am a king. For this reason I was born and I came into the world to bear witness to the truth. Everyone who is of the truth listens to Me."

Pilate said to Him, "What is truth?"

Pilate spoke to the chief priests and the crowd, saying, "I find no guilt in this Man."

Nevertheless, the chief priests and elders accused Him of many things, but He answered nothing. Pilate asked Him again, saying, "Have You no answer? Do You not hear the many things they are testifying against You?" Still Jesus kept silent and said nothing, which greatly impressed the governor, Pilate. They were more emphatic, saying, "He stirs up the people with His teaching throughout all Judea. He began in Galilee and has come to this place."

When Pilate heard that, he asked if the Man was a Galilean. Realizing that He properly came under Herod's jurisdiction, he sent Him to Herod, who was also in Jerusalem at that time.

When Herod saw Jesus, he was very pleased because he had heard much about Him and hoped to see Him do some miracle. He asked Him many questions, but Jesus did not answer anything. The chief priests and religion experts were standing there, vehemently accusing Him.

Herod and his soldiers treated Him with contempt—they mocked Him, dressed Him in a gorgeous robe, and sent Him back to Pilate. That day Herod and Pilate became friends—before they had enmity for each other.

194

Pilate, when he had called together the chief priests, rulers, and the people, said to them, "You brought this Man to me as a disturber of the peace. I examined Him in your presence and found Him not guilty of the things you accused Him of at all. Neither has Herod—he sent Him back to us. He has done nothing that deserves death. I will, therefore, punish Him and then release Him."

At the Feast of Passover, it was the custom of the governor to release a prisoner chosen by the people. At that time they had a notorious prisoner called Barabbas—he was in prison for insurrection in the city, murder during the insurrection, and robbery. The crowd came up and began asking Pilate to do for them as had been his custom. He answered them, saying, "Which do you want me to release to you, Barabbas or Jesus, Who is called Christ, the King of the Jews?" Pilate knew it was because of envy that they had handed Jesus over to him.

While he was sitting on the judgment seat, Pilate's wife sent him a message, saying, "Have nothing to do with that just Man. I have suffered greatly today in a dream because of Him."

Meanwhile, the chief priests and elders persuaded the crowd, stirring them up to have Pilate release Barabbas and to execute Jesus.

The governor said, "It is your custom that I release to you one prisoner at Passover. Which of the two do you want me to release to you? Do you want me to release to you the 'King of the Jews'?"

Then they all shouted back again, saying, "Not Him! Away with Him! Release Barabbas to us!"

Then the governor's soldiers took Jesus into the governor's palace— the Praetorium—and gathered the whole cohort of Roman soldiers. They stripped Him and put on Him a scarlet, purple robe. They twisted together a crown of thorns and put it on His head. They put a reed staff in His right hand. They kneeled before Him and mocked Him, saying, "Hail, King of the Jews!" They struck Him on the head with a reed staff and spit on Him. Kneeling before Him, they mockingly worshiped Him.

Pilate went back out again and said to them, "Behold, I bring Him out to you to let you know that I find Him not guilty of any crime." Then Jesus came out wearing the crown of thorns and the scarlet, purple robe. After they had mocked Him, they took the scarlet, purple robe off Him and put His own clothes on Him.

Pilate said to them, "Behold, here is the Man!"

When the chief priests and guards saw Him, they cried out, saying, "Crucify Him! Crucify Him!"

Pilate said to them, "You take Him and crucify Him. I find no guilt in Him."

The Jews answered, "We have a law and by that law He must die because He claimed to be the Son of God."

When Pilate heard this, he became more afraid. He went back into the judgment hall and said to Jesus, "Where did You come from—to what world do You belong?"

Jesus did not answer him.

Then Pilate said, "You will not speak to me? Do You not know that I have the authority to release You and I have the authority to crucify You?"

Jesus said, "You would not have authority over Me if it had not been given to you from above. For this reason, the one who betrayed Me to you has committed the far greater sin."

At this, Pilate came back out, wanting to release Jesus. He spoke to the crowd, saying, "What shall I do with Jesus Who is called Christ, the One you call the King of the Jews?"

They all shouted, "Let Him be crucified! Crucify Him! Crucify Him!"

For the third time, Pilate spoke to them, saying, "Why? What has He done wrong? I have not found in Him any crime deserving death. Therefore, I will have Him punished and release Him."

The Jews shouted, saying, "If you let this Man go, you are not Caesar's friend. Anyone who makes himself out as a king opposes Caesar."

When Pilate heard this, he brought Jesus outside. He sat down at the judgment seat in a place called the Pavement—in Hebrew, Gabbatha. It was the preparation day for Passover, about the Roman sixth hour (six o'clock in the morning). Pilate said to the Jews, "Here is your King?"

However, they were insistent with loud voices, demanding His crucifixion, shouting, "Let Him be crucified! Crucify Him! Away with Him! Away with Him! Crucify Him!"

Pilate asked, "Shall I crucify your King?"

The chief priests answered, "We have no king except Caesar."

When Pilate saw that he was getting nowhere and that a riot was starting, he took water and washed his hands in the presence of the crowd, saying, "I am innocent of the blood of this Man. You see to it yourselves."

All the people answered, saying, "His blood be on us and our children."

Finally, Pilate, wanting to satisfy the crowd, pronounced sentence granting their demand. He handed Jesus over to them so they could crucify Him. He released Barabbas—the man who had been thrown into prison for insurrection and murder—to them as asked of Pilate. He had Jesus scourged and handed Him over to them for crucifixion. They took Jesus and led Him away to crucify Him.

Jesus' Crucifixion

MATTHEW 27:32–56
MARK 15:21–41
LUKE 23:26–49
JOHN 19:17–37

As they led Jesus away, carrying His own cross, they came on a man from Cyrene named Simon, father of Alexander and Rufus, who was walking by, coming in from the country, and compelled him to carry Jesus' cross behind Him. A large crowd of people followed, including women mourning and lamenting for Him. Jesus turned to the women, saying, "Daughters of Jerusalem, do not cry for Me. Cry for yourselves and for your children. Behold, the time is coming when they will say, 'Blessed are the women who are barren, the wombs that never gave birth, and the breasts that never nursed babies!' Then they will begin to say to the mountains, 'Fall down on us!' and to the hills, 'Cover us!' If people do these things to a green tree, what will they do to a dry tree?" They brought Jesus to the place called the Skull, which, in Hebrew, is called Golgotha. Two other men, both thieves, were taken out with Him to be executed by crucifixion. When they got to the place—called Calvary in Latin—they offered Him wine mixed with gall/myrrh to drink, but when He tasted it, He would not drink it. They crucified Jesus and the two criminals with Him—one to His right, the other to His left, and Jesus in the middle. Jesus prayed, "Father, forgive them; they do not know what they are doing to Me."

When they crucified Him (it was the third hour—nine o'clock in the morning), they took His clothes and divided the outer garments into four parts—one for every soldier. The tunic undergarment was seamless—woven in one piece. Therefore, the soldiers talked to each other, saying, "Let us not tear it, but let us cast lots to decide who will get it." This fulfilled Scripture, which said, "They divided My clothes among them and cast lots for My clothing." Sitting down, they watched over Him.

Standing by the cross of Jesus was His mother, His mother's sister, Mary the wife of Clopas, and Mary Magdalene. When Jesus saw His mother and the disciple whom He loved standing near her, He addressed His mother, saying, "Woman, behold your son!" Then to the disciple He said, "Behold your mother." From that hour that disciple took her into his own home.

Pilate wrote an inscription and had it placed on the cross. Printed on this sign above His head was the accusation against Him: This is Jesus of Nazareth, the King of the Jews. This fulfilled Scripture, which says, "He was numbered with transgressors." This inscription, written in Hebrew, Greek, and Latin, was read by many of the Jews because the place where Jesus was crucified was near the city. The high priests of the Jews said to Pilate, "Do not write 'the King of the Jews'; instead write, 'This Man said I am King of the Jews.'" Pilate answered, saying, "What I have written I have written."

People passing by hurled insults at Him and shook their heads. They said, "Aha! You Who would destroy the temple and then rebuild it in three days, save Yourself! If You are the Son of God, come down from the cross!"

Likewise, the high priests, along with the religion experts and elders, with the people watching, derided Him, saying, "He saved others—He cannot save Himself! Let Him save Himself if He is the Christ, the Chosen One of God! If He is the King of Israel, let Him come down from the cross now and we will believe Him! He trusts in God; let God deliver Him now, if He will have Him—He said, 'I am the Son of God.'" The soldiers also mocked Him—they came up to Him, offering Him sour wine, saying, "If You are the King of the Jews, save Yourself!" The robbers who were crucified with Him mocked and insulted Him in the same way.

Later, one of the criminals hanging there insulted Him, saying, "If You are the Christ, save Yourself and us." However, the other criminal rebuked this robber, saying, "Do you not fear God, since you are under the same sentence? We are justly punished because we receive what we deserve for our actions, but this Man has done nothing wrong." Then he said, "Jesus, remember me when You enter Your kingdom." Jesus said, "Do not worry, I will. Today you will join Me in paradise."

From the sixth hour (noon), darkness came over the whole land until the ninth hour (three o'clock in the afternoon) because of the darkening of the sun's light. About the ninth hour, Jesus cried with a loud voice, saying, "*Eli, Eli, lama sabachthani?*"—which means, "My God, My God, why have You forsaken Me?"

Some bystanders who heard Him said, "This Man is calling for Elijah." After this, Jesus, knowing that all things were now completed, so that Scripture might be fulfilled, said, "I am thirsty." A jar of sour wine vinegar was there. Immediately, one of them ran and took a sponge, soaked it with sour wine vinegar, put it on a stick of hyssop, and gave it to Him to drink. Conversely, the rest of them said, "Let us see if Elijah will come to take Him down to save Him."

When Jesus received the sour wine vinegar, He cried out again in a loud voice, saying, "It is finished. Father, into Your hands I commit My spirit."

At that moment, the sanctuary curtain was ripped in two, from top to bottom. The earth shook and rocks were split in pieces. Graves were opened up and many bodies of the saints, which slept in death, were raised to life. After Jesus' resurrection, they entered the holy city and appeared to many people.

The Roman centurion and those who were with him standing guard in front of Jesus were very frightened when they saw the earthquake, and everything else that was happening, and how Jesus died, said, "This Man was righteous and innocent! Truly this Man was the Son of God!"

All who had come to see this spectacle, when they saw what took place, beat their breasts with grief and returned home. All of Jesus' acquaintances, along with the women who had followed Him from Galilee, stood at a distance watching these things. Among them were Mary Magdalene, Mary the mother of the younger James and Joses, and Salome, the mother of the Zebedee sons. When Jesus was in Galilee, these women followed and ministered to Him. There were many other women who had come up with Him to Jerusalem.

Then the Jews, since it was the Day of Preparation and so the bodies would not remain on the crosses on the Sabbath day—it was a high holy day that year—requested Pilate to have their legs broken to speed death and to have the bodies taken down. So the soldiers came and broke the legs of the first man crucified with Jesus and then the other. When they came to Jesus and saw that He was already dead, they did not break His legs. Nevertheless, one of the soldiers pierced His side with his spear. Immediately, blood and water gushed out. The eyewitness to these things gives this evidence and his testimony is true. He is telling the truth so that you, also, will believe. These things were done to fulfill Scripture, which says, "Not one of His bones will be broken," and, "They shall look on the One they pierced," as it says in another Scripture.

Jesus' Burial

MATTHEW 27:57–66
MARK 15:42–47
LUKE 23:50–56
JOHN 19:38–42

After this, when it was evening, since it was the day before the Sabbath and the Day of Preparation—the Sabbath was about to begin—a rich man from the Jewish town of Arimathea and a disciple of Jesus—but secretly because he feared the Jews—arrived at the site. His name was Joseph, a respected member of the Sanhedrin council. He was waiting for the kingdom of God. He was a good and righteous man; he had not consented to the plans and actions of the council. He went boldly to Pilate and asked for Jesus' body. Pilate wondered if He could be dead so soon. Therefore, he called the centurion and asked him if Jesus was already dead. When he was told by the centurion that He was dead, he ordered the body be given to Joseph, who then came and took away His body.

Joseph bought a fine linen cloth. Then he took Jesus' body down. Nicodemus—who at first had come to Jesus by night—was with him and brought a mixture of myrrh and aloes that weighed seventy-five to one hundred pounds. They took Jesus' body and wrapped it in strips of the fine linen cloth with the spices in accordance with the Jewish burial custom. There was a garden near the place He was crucified and in the garden a new tomb, which had been hewn out of a rock and in which no one had ever been laid—the tomb belonged to Joseph. Since it was the Jewish Day of Preparation and the Sabbath was drawing near, they laid Jesus there because it was conveniently nearby. They rolled a large stone against the entrance to the tomb and departed from there.

The women who had come with Jesus from Galilee had followed them, saw the tomb and how the body was laid in it—Mary Magdalene and the other Mary, mother of Joses, were sitting opposite the tomb and watched the burial. Then they went back to prepare burial spices and perfumes. They rested quietly on the Sabbath, according to the commandment.

The next day—the day after the Day of Preparation—the high priests and Pharisees came before Pilate, saying, "We remember that deceiver, while He was still alive, said, 'After three days I will rise again.' Command, therefore, that the tomb be made secure until the third day lest His disciples come by night, steal Him away, and say to the people, 'He has risen from the dead.' If this happens, the last deception will be worse than the first."

Pilate said to them, "You have a guard. Go and make it as secure as you can." So they went and made the tomb secure by sealing the stone and posting guards.

Chapter 9

RESURRECTION OF JESUS

Jesus' Resurrection

MATTHEW 28:1–15
MARK 16:1–11
LUKE 24:1–12
JOHN 20:1–18

After the Sabbath, Mary Magdalene, Mary the mother of James, and Salome brought sweet spices so that they might come and anoint Jesus' body. Very early in the morning, on the first day of the week, while it was still dark and the dawn started at the rising of the sun, Mary Magdalene, the other Mary, and other women went to look at the tomb—they brought the spices they had prepared earlier.

They said to each other, "Who will roll away the stone from the entrance of the tomb for us?" There was a great earthquake—an angel of the Lord descended from heaven, came to the tomb, rolled the stone from the entrance, and sat on it. When the women looked up, they saw that the stone, which was very large, rolled away. The angel's appearance was like lightning and his clothes were white as snow. The tomb guards were so afraid at the sight of him that they shook and became like dead men.

The women entered the tomb and did not find the body of the Lord Jesus. While they were perplexed about this, suddenly two men—angels—in dazzling clothes were by them; one was standing and the other was sitting on the right side. The women were amazed and afraid. This caused them to bow their faces to the ground. However, the angel sitting on the right side said to the women, "Do not be afraid. I know you are looking for Jesus of Nazareth, the One they crucified on the cross. Why are you looking for the living One among the dead? He is not here but has risen just as He said. Come and look at the place where the Lord lay. See the place where they laid Him. Remember how He told you when He was still in Galilee, saying, 'The Son of Man must be delivered into the hands of sinful men, be crucified, and the third day rise again'?" Then they remembered His words. The angel said, "Go quickly; tell His disciples and Peter that He is risen from the dead and is going ahead of you to Galilee. There you will see Him. I have told you just as He said to you." Again they remembered His words.

The women quickly departed trembling and running from the tomb with fear and great joy. They said nothing to anyone because of their fear. They ran to tell all these things to Simon Peter, the one Jesus loved, the rest of the eleven apostles, and all the other disciples. They said, "They took the Lord from the tomb and we do not know where they have laid Him!"

However, Mary had stayed behind and stood crying outside the tomb. As she wept, she knelt to look into the tomb and saw two angels sitting there, dressed in white, one at the head and the other at the foot of where Jesus' body had been laid. They said to her, "Woman, why do you cry?" She said, "I cry because they have taken away my Lord and I do not know where they have laid Him." (After rising from the dead, Jesus appeared early on Sunday morning to Mary Magdalene, whom He had delivered from seven demons.) After she said this, she turned around and saw Jesus standing there, but she did not recognize Him. Jesus said to her, "Woman, why do you cry? Whom do you seek?" She, supposing that He was the gardener, said, "Sir, if you have carried Him away from here, tell me where You laid Him and I will take Him away." Jesus said to her, "Mary." She turned toward Him and said to Him in Hebrew, "*Rabboni!*" (which means Teacher or Master). Jesus said to her, "Do not touch Me because I have not yet ascended to My Father. Go to My brothers and tell them, 'I ascend to My Father and your Father, to My God and your God.'"

After that, when some of the other women were running from the tomb to tell His disciples, Jesus met them, saying, "Greetings." They came to Him, held His feet, and worshiped Him. Then Jesus said to them, "Do not be afraid. Go tell My brothers to go to Galilee and there they will see Me."

Mary Magdalene came and told the disciples, who were mourning and weeping, that she had seen the Lord. She told them everything He said to her. When they heard that she had seen Him alive, they did not believe her.

Peter and the other disciple got up and ran to the tomb. They ran together, but the other disciple got to the tomb first, outrunning Peter. Stooping down and looking in, he saw the linen cloths lying there, but he did not go in. Then Simon Peter, arriving after him, entered the tomb, saw the linen cloths lying there and the napkin, used to cover His head, not lying with the linen cloths but rolled up in a place by itself. Then the other disciple, the one who got to the tomb first, went in, saw, and believed what the women said. They still did not understand from the Scripture that He had to rise from the dead. Peter went away wondering about these things.

Mary Magdalene, Joanna, Mary the mother of James, and the other women with them kept telling the things that happened at the tomb to the apostles. They did not believe a word of it and thought they were making it all up. Then the disciples went back again to their own homes.

Meanwhile, while the women were going to tell the disciples, some of the guards went into the city and told the high priests everything that had happened to them. They called a meeting of the elders and consulted together. They gave a large sum of money to the soldiers, saying, "You are to say, 'His disciples came at night and stole Him away while we were asleep.' If the governor hears this, we will persuade him and keep you out of trouble." The soldiers took the money and did as they were instructed by the elders. This story was widely spread among the Jews to the present day.

Emmaus Appearance

MARK 16:12
LUKE 24:13–32

Later that same day, He appeared in a different form to two of them as they were walking in the countryside to a town called Emmaus, which was about sixty furlongs (about seven miles) from Jerusalem. They talked together about all these things that had happened recently. It came to pass that, while they were conversing and discussing with each other, Jesus came up and walked along with them, but their eyes were prevented from recognizing Him.

Jesus asked them, "What is this you are discussing between you as you walk along?"

They stopped walking and looked sad. Then one of them, his name was Cleopas, said to Him, "Are You the only stranger in Jerusalem Who does not know the things that have occurred in these days?"

Jesus said, "What things?"

They said, "The things concerning Jesus of Nazareth, Who was a Prophet, mighty in deed and word before God and all the people. The high priests and our rulers delivered Him to be condemned to death and crucified Him. We were hoping that He was the One Who would redeem and free Israel. It is now the third day since these things were done. Moreover, some of our women have astonished us. Early this morning they were at the tomb but did not find His body. They came back saying that they had seen a vision of angels who said He was alive. Some of those with us went to the tomb and found it empty just as the women said, but they did not see Jesus."

Then He said to them, "How foolish you are and how slow of heart to believe everything the prophets have spoken! Was it not necessary for the Christ to suffer these things before entering His glory?" Beginning with Moses and then with the prophets, He explained to them in all the Scriptures the things concerning Himself.

As they came near the town where they were going, He acted as if He was going on farther. They urged Him, saying, "It is nearly evening and the day is nearly over! Stay with us." Jesus went in to stay with them.

It came to pass that, as He reclined at the table with them, He took bread, blessed it, broke it, and gave it to them. At that moment their eyes were opened and they recognized Him. Then He vanished from their sight. They said to one another, "Did our hearts not burn within us while He talked with us, as we walked, as He explained the Scriptures to us?"

No Ghost

MARK 16:13
LUKE 24:33–43
JOHN 20:19–23

The two of them got up and immediately returned to Jerusalem. When it was evening of that first day of the week, the disciples were assembled behind locked doors for fear of the Jews. There they found the Eleven and those who were with them. They were saying, "The Lord is risen indeed. He has appeared to Simon." Then the two men told what had happened when they were walking and how they recognized Jesus when He broke the bread.

While they were saying all this, Jesus came, stood among them, and said, "Peace be with you!" When He had said this, He showed them His hands and His side. The disciples were joyful when they saw the Lord. Then Jesus said to them again, "Peace be with you! Just as the Father has sent Me, I am sending you." However, they were startled and frightened—they thought they were seeing a ghost. He continued, saying, "Why are you disturbed and why do doubts arise in your hearts?

Look at My hands and My feet. It is I, Myself! Touch Me and see; a ghost does not have flesh and bones; I do, as you can see." When He had said this, He showed them His hands and feet. While they still could not believe it because of joy and wonder, He asked them, "Have you anything here to eat?" They gave Him a piece of broiled fish and a honeycomb. He took it and ate it in front of them.

When He had said this, He breathed on them and said, "Receive the Holy Spirit. If you forgive anyone his sins, they are forgiven. If you do not forgive the sins of anyone, they are not forgiven."

Prophecy Witnesses

LUKE 24:44–49

Then He said to them, "I told you while I was still with you that everything must be fulfilled that was written about Me in the law of Moses, the prophets, and psalms."

Then He thoroughly opened their minds so they could understand the Scriptures. He said to them, "It is written the Christ should suffer and should rise from the dead on the third day; repentance and forgiveness of sins will be preached in His name among all nations, beginning at Jerusalem. You are witnesses of these things. I am sending what My Father promised to you, but stay in the city of Jerusalem until you have been clothed with power from on high."

Thomas Doubts

JOHN 20:24–31

However, Thomas, one of the Twelve called Didymus (the Twin), was not with them when Jesus appeared to them. The other disciples told him, "We have seen the Lord!"

In spite of this, he said to them, "Unless I see the nail holes in His hands, put my finger in the nail holes, and put my hand in His side, I will not believe it."

Eight days later, His disciples were again in the house and Thomas was with them. Jesus came, even though the doors were locked, and stood among them. He said, "Peace to you!" Then He spoke to Thomas, saying, "Reach your finger and examine My hands. Reach your hand and put it in My side. Stop your unbelief and believe."

Thomas said to Him, "My Lord and my God!"

Jesus said, "You believe because you have seen Me. Blessed are those who believe even though they have not seen Me."

Jesus performed many other miracles in the presence of His disciples that are not written in this book. These are written down so that you may believe that Jesus is the Christ, the Son of God, and so that by believing you may have life through His name.

Fish Breakfast

JOHN 21:1–14

After this, Jesus appeared again to His disciples at the Sea of Tiberias. This is how He showed Himself: Simon Peter, Thomas called Didymus (the Twin), Nathanael from Cana in Galilee, the sons of Zebedee, and two other of His disciples were together. Simon Peter said to them, "I am going fishing." They replied, "We are coming with you!" They went out and got in the boat. They caught nothing that night.

When the morning sun came up, Jesus stood on the beach, but they did not know it was Him. So Jesus said to them, "Children, did you catch any fish?"

They answered, "No."

He said, "Cast the net off the right side of the boat and you will find some." They did this and now were unable to haul it in because of the large number of fish.

Then the disciple Jesus loved said to Peter, "It is the Lord!" When Simon Peter heard that it was the Lord, he put on his fisherman's coat—he was naked—and jumped into the sea. The other disciples came in by small boat; they were not far from shore—about two hundred cubits (a hundred yards)—dragging the net full of fish. When they got out on the beach, they saw a fire of coals there, fish laid on it, and some bread.

Jesus said to them, "Bring some of the fish you have just caught."

Simon Peter went aboard and pulled the net to shore—153 large fish! Even with all those fish, the net was not torn. Jesus said to them, "Come and have breakfast." Not one of the disciples dared ask, "Who are You?" They knew it was the Lord. Jesus then came, took the bread, and gave it to them. He did the same with the fish. This was now the third time that Jesus showed Himself to the disciples after He had risen.

Love Me?

JOHN 21:15–25

When they had eaten, Jesus said to Simon Peter, "Simon, son of John, do you love Me more than these?"

Peter replied, "Yes, Lord, You know that I love You."

Jesus said, "Feed My lambs."

He then asked a second time, "Simon, son of John, do you love Me?"

Peter replied, "Yes, Lord, You know I love You."

Jesus said, "Take care of My sheep."

Then a third time He said, "Simon, son of John, do you love Me?"

Peter was grieved that He for a third time asked, "Do you love Me?" He answered, "Lord, You know all things. You know that I love You."

Jesus said, "Feed My sheep. I tell you the truth, when you were young you dressed yourself and went wherever you pleased, but when you get old, you will have to stretch out your hands while someone else dresses you and takes you where you do not want to go." Jesus said this to signify the kind of death by which Peter would glorify God. Then He said to him, "Follow Me."

Then Peter turned and saw the disciple whom Jesus loved following them—this is the one who leaned on Jesus' chest at the supper and who said, "Who is it that is going to betray You?" When Peter saw him, he said to Jesus, "Lord, what about this man?"

Jesus said, "If I want him to live until I come again, what is that to you? You follow Me!" That is how the rumor got out among the brothers that this disciple would not die. However, Jesus did not say that he would not die. He simply said, "If I want him to live until I come again, what is that to you?"

This is the disciple who is testifying to these things and wrote them down. We know that his testimony is true.

There are also many other things Jesus did that, if they were all written down, I suppose that even the world could not contain the books that would be written about them.

Great Commission

MATTHEW 28:16–20

Then the eleven disciples went to Galilee, to the mountain Jesus had directed them. When they saw Him they worshiped Him, but some had doubt.

Jesus came up and said to them, "All authority has been given to Me in heaven and on earth. Go, therefore, and make disciples of all nations, baptizing them in the name of the Father, Son, and Holy Spirit. Teach them to obey everything I have commanded you. Lo, I am with you always, even to the end of the age."

Disciples Commissioned

MARK 16:14–18

Still later, as the Eleven were eating, Jesus appeared and reproached them for their unbelief and hardness of heart because they refused to believe those who had seen Him after He was raised from the dead. Then He said, "Go into all the world and preach the Gospel—the good news—to all human creation. Whoever believes and is baptized will be saved, but whoever does not believe will be condemned eternally. These signs will accompany believers: They will drive out demons in My name; they will speak in new languages; they will pick up snakes with their hands; they will drink deadly poison but it will not hurt them; they will lay hands on the sick and make them well."

Jesus' Ascension

MARK 16:19–20
LUKE 24:50–53

Jesus then led them out as far as Bethany. After the Lord Jesus had spoken to them, He lifted His hands and blessed them. While He blessed them, He left them—He was taken up into heaven and sat at the right hand of God. Then the disciples worshiped Him and returned to Jerusalem with great joy. They were continually in the temple praising and blessing God. They went everywhere preaching, while the Lord kept working with them and confirming His word with signs and miracles that accompanied it. Amen.

INDEX OF SCRIPTURE
PASSAGES

INDEX OF SCRIPTURE PASSAGES

LaVergne, TN USA
09 March 2010
175317LV00002B/6/P

9 781414 109084